HUMOROUS STORIES FROM THE U.P. HUNTING CAMPS

Each story is a true experience written in the humorous way of the Yooper!!

By the U.P. Rabbit
Robert R. Hruska

Humorous Stories from the U.P. Deer Camps

First Edition: 1999
Copyright © 1998
ISBN # 0-9668265-0-7

Published by
McNaughton & Gunn, Inc.
960 Woodlawn Drive
Saline, Michigan 48176

All inquires should be addressed to:
Robert R. Hruska, Author
140 S Birch Avenue
Gillett, Wisconsin 54124
Phone: (920) 855-2996

Illustrations by:
Brian Fretig, Teacher, Sportsman, and Friend

Dedication

To my parents, Bill and Mildred Hruska who instilled the love of the outdoors in me through many family hunting and fishing trips and family life at the camp. To my brother, Bill, who shared in most of these experiences; my wife, Barbara, for believing that I'd finish this book; and my sons, Randy and Wayne for your support and just being there.

Table of Contents

CHAPTER 1

HUNTING WITH HARRY
Armed and Dangerous!

All of us have done something dangerous in our lifetime. I hunted one season with Harry. He was ARMED AND DANGEROUS with a new 270 rifle and scope. He had never hunted before, and I doubt if he even tried out that rifle before coming to camp. This 270 was his deer rifle where we normally shoot at a distance of 50 to 75 yards for our deer.

Harry did odd things before WITHOUT a rifle. We didn't trust him then, let alone now when he had this, "I can shoot through the whole cedar swamp" attitude.

He came up to our deer camp as a "semi-invited, relative" member. Three days before the season, his wife called and asked if he could hunt with us. My wife took the call and couldn't say no. By now, you probably guessed that he wouldn't be our first pick of camping partners.

He arrived at camp in his pickup truck, opened the door, and a very clean pie-tin fell out of the door. We didn't think anything of it until after the season. His wife asked us how we liked the apple pie that she made and sent up for us. He must have polished that one off on the way up. The pan was so shiny, you'd have thought that a bear had licked it clean.

Well, he came into camp with his rifle, clothes and an appetite that wouldn't quit. As Bill said, "He doesn't refuse any food. Holy Wah! He must weigh 390# standing on his hind legs." We wouldn't normally have been concerned about his weight, but we weren't set up for someone with his appetite.

At one meal, he ate everything left over except a half loaf of bread that had blue mold on it. We told him that the bread mold is what they make penicillin out of and it's healthy for you. He looked at it kind of suspicious and then ate that too.

We had camp groceries bought for two weeks and with a little common sense, always had more than enough for everyone. We had all of the important stuff like, beer, brandy, six quarts of tomato juice for Bloody Marys and the groceries.

The second evening, about 8:00 p.m., we started to play cards. Harry said he was not interested in playing so he was walking around inside the camp doing nothing in particular. Suddenly, we heard, "Glug, glug, glug!" coming from the supply room. Bob jumped up from the game and looked. . . . He said, "Now he's killing the tomato juice." Bob took the second quart away from him. He had already drank a quart and a half.

We were getting nervous. He already ate well for two or three people and couldn't seem to quit. We knew we needed to depend on the grocery supply. After all, we had to save the extra funds for refreshments which always seemed to run out. We didn't care to waste it on more groceries, especially when you couldn't predict they would last even two days.

There were four of us in camp. We other three, started to brainstorm how we could solve this problem. Some of the ideas that I remember were:

1. Take him WAY out into the woods and lose him. Then we thought that wouldn't work. He was bound to find his way back somehow and would only be twice as hungry when he returned.

2. Put some X-lax in his food and teach him a lesson. Then we figured he'd be so cleaned out that he might eat like a bear. We did smile a lot on that one though.

3. Pour some chocolate over a few yeast cakes. We were convinced that he'd eat anything!

Bob said, "Look, we've got more rutabagas than we can ever feed the deer, let's cook up a batch of those for him. Like you say, he'll eat anything!"

We thought that we'd start with the rutabaga idea first and could work our way up to the others if we had to. He LIKED them! He even said that they were good cold.

Now, our camp beds all have used, squeaky springs on them. We all heard him roll out at night—SQUEAK!—turn on his flashlight and go to the toilet. We also heard a suspicious rattling of paper and noticed half of the cookie supply was missing in the morning.

The next night, Harry turned over to get out of his bed—SCREECH—went the springs in his bed. SCREECH, SCREECH, SCREECH, came from the other three beds as everyone sat up with their flashlights on. Bill said, "We'll give you a little light until you get back." You could hear him grumbling to himself and Bill then said, "Guys, we've got to think of something else. That gas he's making from all those rutabagas is really getting to me."

It was easy to agree with that! We started to plan again. "Let's take him into the woods and lose him. Let's go into town and get a dozen loaves of that week old bread. He even ate the stuff that turned blue before. I'd like to give him the X-lax. You guys only THINK that could hurt him. I don't think anything would hurt him."

We needed to cut more fire wood in the second week. Harry said, "I thought that you guys had plenty of wood cut for the season." We didn't, so we all got started on the woodpile. I noticed Harry quitting a lot and going out to the outhouse a lot. He was hitting the ground about every five feet on the run. It looked unusual to see someone so big run so fast.

As we watched him, I said, "One of you slipped him the X-lax didn't you?" EVERYONE smiled and said, YEAH! On his last run, he said, "Guys, I'm sorry but I can't help with the wood. These rutabagas seem to have given me the diarrhea."

After he went back inside, I said, "And you know, now he wants to go on our Canadian fly-in fishing trip with us. How are we going to pack enough groceries? Dave said, "Don't worry about the groceries. If he goes all we need is a little X-lax and a lot more toilet paper."

Another quirk, he never liked to walk very far and got bored quickly with most anything if there was no quick action with it. He'd think nothing of lining up on a squirrel and shooting at it after sitting on a deer post for a few hours. If he missed, he'd shoot 2-3 times. We tried to put him on a post anticipating something like this. He may scare the deer toward us.

That year, we were making big deer drives. We had 10 drivers and 10 posters (shooters on the stand). The drivers were walking in one long column, single file, to go to their positions when we noticed Harry, who was third in line, with his gun safety off and pointing his gun wherever it pointed. We quickly promoted him to the front of the column and everyone stayed directly behind him. He didn't care for that as he never liked to be corrected.

That afternoon, we took a group break from the deer drive. We sat in a good sized circle facing each other. About five minutes into the break, a huge-racked buck came out of nowhere and almost ran into our circle, then turned and ran away. Harry jumped up and shot from the hip over everyone's head at it. None of us moved for about a minute. You kind of looked around to see if you had a hole in yourself somewhere. The group very soberly agreed that we had enough driving for that day and would go back to our own camps. I got the word on the way out of the words. "If you guys expect to join us again, don't bring that Harry."

Guys like Harry are the kind that see things that the average hunter never has the opportunity to see. It just seems to happen that way. How many hunters actually get to see deer mating? Harry did. He was sitting on a deer stand pretty well covered with evergreen boughs. In fact, it was hard to see out of that blind.

Harry told us that he was sitting there for about an hour when he heard sounds behind him. He said it sounded like someone watching fireworks go off into the air. You know, like "Oooooh! Ahhhh! Oooooh! Ahhhh! And, he said, that was only the doe! He didn't get a shot or he didn't think to shoot. Harry was a hero with that story. He added more sounds every time that he told it. We were all careful that he wasn't holding his gun, though, when he did.

After telling that story, he told us casually, that he was going home that night. Life can be hard on a lonely hunter.

CHAPTER 2

JOSEPH
A Most Unforgettable Character

He was like a Pied Piper in our end of the town. All of
the kids knew that wherever he went, something BIG
normally happened. It wasn't stealing, break-ins or
such, but more of the devilish type things.

He seemed to draw the neighborhood kids like a
magnet to wait and watch for something to happen.
The neighborhood mothers seemed to hate him as
much as the kids loved him. Any kid that went
anywhere with him normally came back home wet to
the waist from chasing molting ducks, black clothes
from being at the dump, or just dirty, in general.

Joseph was slim built, slow and deliberate moving.
He rarely smiled or laughed, and when he would say,
"Hello!" to you, his voice seemed to have ice in it, . . .
cold and sober. The neighborhood ladies would
cringe when he'd walk by. We never quite knew why.
Maybe it was because of his pet skunk that always
followed about ten feet behind him.

One lady, I thought, went a little above and beyond.
She came out of her house one day when they were
walking by and pet the skunk. I remember she said,
"what a nice pet. Did it bother the skunk when you
had it spaded?" (Spaded = so it cannot spray its'
scent) Joseph looked at her real serious and said,

"What do you mean by spaded?" The lady looked back at Joseph and I swear, her eyes got bigger and bigger. She started to scream and ran for her house, hitting the ground about ever five feet. Her arms were extended out as far as they would go and at the same time, she was shaking her hands back and forth as fast as she could. She screamed and screamed all the way into her house and slammed the door.

Now, what kid wouldn't want to follow Joseph around and see a sight like that? None of us were really sure if he had that skunk spaded or if they just had an understanding between each other. I never did see anyone else but him pet it. Joseph followed his own drummer in life. Whatever he wanted to do, within reason, and if it looked like he could get away with it, he'd do it.

His skunk liked live food so Joseph would catch frogs, cut off their legs to eat himself and give the rest to his skunk. I saw him going past our house one day, carrying a large paper bag that was jumping up and down as he carried it. I said, "It looks like Joseph caught something to feed to his skunk." I can remember my mother saying, "Get away from that window!" She didn't appreciate him like we did.

He was also quite a woodsman. He loved hunting and would hunt anything. I'm sure he shot whatever animal roamed the woods in Menominee County and ate it. He never wasted anything but just about lived on wild game.

Joseph took great pride in never moving when he went posting for deer. Most hunters sit in a nice blind when posting for deer. Not Joseph. He would truly STAND in one position for hours and never move his feet when posting. One time, I came upon him in the woods posting and he was covered with about three inches of fresh snow. He never moved to wipe it off. If it wasn't for parts of the orange jacket showing, you wouldn't have seen him.

It would not be natural, that a guy like this would some day attract the attention of a game warden. One year, a warden accused him of shooting a farmer's cow, taking the hind quarters and covering up the rest with brush. This happened about 10 miles from Joseph's camp so I suppose, who else would you logically accuse? It was never proven so he didn't seem to be upset.

He did say to me a few weeks later, "Damn cow beef taste a lot better than venison." That's one of the few times that I saw him smile.

When he'd go hunting, he'd walk backwards through the snow to go off of a road. It'd look like he came TO the road rather than walking away from it. There was no real need to do this. It was just part of his nature.

Some days, we'd go to the dumps and shoot rats. Joseph wondered if he skinned the big ones if he could sell them as squirrels to someone. He had a friend that raised tame rabbits and sold them to customers. One year, this friend ran out of rabbits and people kept asking him for more. He then started to trap the stray neighborhood cats, skin and clean them and sold them for rabbits. The customers said those rabbits were real tasty and wanted more. Joseph admired that guy.

Well, life of a kid like this didn't go unnoticed by the local police patrolling the town. One individual took particular attention in zeroing in on Joseph regularly to the point that it annoyed him. One day, he saw this particular police car parked where he could safely visit it. He wired a fresh road-kill skunk on top of the car's muffler! Talk about a stink! I'm sure they put a new muffler on that car. It was very noticeable that this policeman made a wide circle thereafter whenever he saw Joseph. He wasn't sure, but he wasn't taking any chances.

I saw Joseph again a few years ago. He returned to the hometown for a funeral. We had a long visit and he introduced me to his wife. She was beautiful! Shapely, personable, and a very nice person. After she visited with me, I commented to him that I thought she was an exceptionally nice person. (Besides, who in their wildest dreams would have expected that such a fine lady would consent to marrying Joseph?) His remark back to me was very sober as was his nature, "I'm going to divorce her next year. I'm going to move back into Menominee County and she doesn't want to leave the big city where we live now. If she won't move, she's of no use to me." I looked across the room at her, where she was visiting so nicely with other ladies. I'm sure she had no idea that he had this in mind.

These were the ways of Joseph.

CHAPTER 3

OUR FIRST DEER CAMP

You always remember your first deer camp. That's where activities before the season got a young kid all bug-eyed with excitement in waiting and wondering what would happen next.

We built that camp out of all used lumber. That's what hunters could afford at that time and it seemed to be the standard. We used no power tools, no electricity, no insulation, nothing but the bare necessities. Someone posted a sign inside the camp that said, "If you don't see it, we ain't got it. If we ain't got it, we don't want it." That seemed to be the general spirit. If you could endure with what we had, you accomplished something.

The camp was one large room with double bunks, stacked two high, so it slept four. There was a wood cooking stove and an old oil heater. When the heater was started, it would make sounds steady at night, like, "Glub, glub, glub-glub, glub-glub, glub-woosh!" Compare this sound to a dripping faucet when you're trying to sleep.

The "glub-woosh" happened about once every five minutes when a bigger shot of oil got through to the burner and made this mild explosion as it burned. The heater accomplished two things: first it made you think you were, in time, going to get warmer, and second, it kept the frost off of itself.

Sleeping double in each bunk did more to keep us warm than the heater. I won't say it was the coldest camp in the county, but our rubber boots (that had a little snow on them when you went to bed) would freeze to the floor by morning.

The wood cook stove didn't seem to throw off much heat either as it went out quickly after the meal was made. I watched a mouse run the full length on top of the stove pipe without getting burned. It couldn't have hurt itself as I saw it do this twice.

We'd play cards until about 2:00 a.m. in the morning with a Coleman gas lantern hanging above the table for light. Depending upon where you were sitting under it, you could either see pretty good or had to do a powerful squint.

The gas lantern needed to be repumped up with air about every half hour so it would burn brighter. Towards the end of the evening, no one would make a move to repump the lanterns, hoping someone else would do it. In this stage of its going dimmer, the lantern would burn bright, then dim, then bright, then dim, every few seconds.

The card players had a tendency to move their heads to the action of the lantern: bright—they'd subconsciously move their heads 2-3 inches backward, dim—they'd move their heads 2-3 inches forward. Picture this constant back and forth movement until the lantern was finally repumped by someone and it would burn steady again. It kind of reminded you of a barn yard chicken moving its head back and forth.

The cards were always a "found" deck. No one ever bought any. They "found" this used deck somewhere. As a result, they didn't slide too good and had a tendency to stick to each other. One older camp member discovered a way to cure this. He put cooking flour on the table to make them slide better. (Like putting a compound on a dance floor to make your feet slide better.)

The idea worked, but in no time our hands and arms were white with flour. If you scratched yourself anywhere, you'd have a white spot of flour there, too.

One night, during one of these games, there was a knock on the door and a game warden stepped in. He looked at everyone around that card table bobbing their heads, three inches forward and three inches back, the light flickering bright and dim at the same time, all the players by now almost covered with white flour, and he took a step backward. He must have thought that he stumbled into some kind of a new religious cult. He said, "I'm not staying too long," and kind of sat against the wall near the door.

When he left, the talk swung over to game wardens. Uncle Al said, "I never did like game wardens. They always seem to be sneaking around making you feel uncomfortable." We never had any problems with them because we all would shoot only bucks. "But," he continued, "ONE day, there will be a new hunter here that probably will not get a buck and cause them to bother us." I could feel everyone looking at me, the guy that never fired a shot yet, at a deer.

When I closed my eyes to sleep that night, I could feel my head bobbing from the light, remember how everyone looked at me, and dreamed of a game warden chasing me with a rope.

You could lay in the top bunk and watch partridge walking the length of tree branches about 20 feet behind the camp. Then you'd hear the older guys get up to go relieve themselves outside, not knowing how lucky you were to have younger and stronger "plumbing" as they called it.

Then, it wasn't too long and Dad would get up, make a fire in the cook stove and start making breakfast. I'd lay still with my eyes closed hoping no one would roust me out in the cold to go and get more firewood.

Soon, the camp would warm up about 10 degrees and you felt warmer. Someone would say, "Next year, we should get some insulation in this camp." Grandpa would say, "That's for sissies. All you've got to do is have some hot coffee." You could usually see your breath as they were talking.

The stories that came in from the hunt was really part of the exciting camp life. It seemed that you could stretch the truth telling them as long as they were reasonable.

Later in the evening, we'd go "camp hopping" to see how the other camps were doing. One camp that we visited said, "Next year, we're going to have insulation for sure." I said, without thinking, "That's for sissies."

Dad looked at me and grinned. I asked him, "what was the matter?" He said, "Wait until your mother sees you after two weeks up here. You look two shades darker and smell like the rest of us." He always had the philosophy that, "The apple doesn't fall very far from the tree." He felt that this experience taught character, perseverance, and a hearty personality.

I thought about that and then was really proud. It was like an earned badge of honor. Like being accepted into the veteran hunters' group.

I froze, bobbed my head, gradually got dirtier, picked up a lot of odd quirks, and felt good! I lived through it! What makes a real Yooper? These were all traits developed in life that you never forget.

CHAPTER 4

TANGLING WITH GAME WARDENS

Each one that I've met was always different. It seemed that the older they were, the more common sense they used. The young ones seem to be "by the book" and used more absolute judgment. The older ones looked for "extenuating circumstances" before making their decisions.

Dad used to say, "The good ones went to see God on Sunday. The bad ones thought that they were God." It doesn't take long when a new, assigned warden has a reasonable or unworthy reputation passed onto him by all the sportsmen in the county. His first one or two judgments would quickly be passed along in the taverns or work places.

One of the first wardens that I remember, was a man named Rose working out of Menominee. Dad found a hen pheasant one day with a broken wing. It appeared like someone had shot it. He put it out of its misery and by accident, found Rose on patrol. He reported it to him and told him what he had done. Rose thought for awhile and sized us up. He must have felt that we didn't waste much at the table and gave it back to Dad to eat.

Another experience, I was later fishing in our 14 foot boat with my wife and two small boys. Two, young, wardens pulled up along side, put some long handled boat hooks onto our boat to hold us to theirs. There was no current and we were only a foot apart. I said that I'd hold onto their boat if they wanted but I didn't think it was necessary to clamp onto us. (They met us as friends and suddenly we became captives.) They said, "No, we always do this and then have no problems with anyone." They didn't show much 'people sense.' I wondered if they thought that my wife and kids were a threat to them.

A good friend of mine told me a story about another warden. My friend was from Niagara, Wisconsin and he would bring his rabbit hound across the river into Michigan to a close swamp to train it for rabbit hunting. The dog drove a rabbit past him this one day, and he shot it. A while later, a game warden drove up to him standing by his car and asked if his dog was driving the swamp. Gene said, "I couldn't deny it because he had my dog in his back seat." Gene said he had a real hollow feeling. The warden asked him to see his license and he had to tell him he didn't have any, that he normally just came here to train his dog. The warden looked him over and said, "How would you like to buy one?" He bought one from the warden and every year thereafter, took his dog into Michigan but said, "I always bought a license and I'll never forget that game warden."

There was one in the Escanaba area that liked to literally jump out in front of a hunter's moving car on single lane roads to check for violations. One day, he did this and was run over. Makes you wonder, what was gained by that logic?

I met another one, two years ago. He was watching fishermen way out on the ice off of the Menominee lighthouse. This was in the Spring of the year and the ice really looked unsafe. He said, "I'm concerned about those guys fishing out of their cars way out there. I'll sit here awhile in case they need help." I thought, what a nice attitude toward some foolish fishermen.

Three years ago, I was in a fishing group of four on a fly-in trip out of WaWa, Canada. We flew for about an hour into the "Boonies," landed onto a lake and were the only group in this remote, road-less spot for a week. On the day that we were due to leave, about noon, a game warden came onto our cabin porch and knocked on the door. We couldn't have been less shocked if it was a grizzly bear. Where did he come from? He didn't want to talk but wanted to check our limits of fish. He said it took him half a day to portage into our lake and demanded to see our fish.

We had the exact limits we were allowed, packed and ready to take home. He counted those, looked inside them for smaller ones, searched the entire cabin, the oven of the stove, etc. and didn't find any more. Then he checked in both boats for a "dead floater." (When the boat has a few inches of water in it, sometimes you catch a trout, it gets away from you in the boat, dies, and may "float" under the boat seat and float back out.) We worried there for a minute, because that could happen to anyone.

He looked UNDER our garbage bag we had set by the dock to take back out, then said he was going to make a circle in the woods around the cabin to check for litter. Vic, one of our guys said, "I think he's looking for a hidden cooler of fish." We didn't have any of that so we weren't worried. When he returned, we offered him a cup of coffee and he sat down very noticeably nervous. He said, "You're the first party of fishermen to use this camp that I didn't arrest for having too many fish." He then jumped up from his seat like he was stuck with a pin and said, "Do you have another boat out fishing, yet?" We didn't. Then we adjusted ourselves (relaxed) toward him and asked him friendly questions, like, "Do you like being a game warden? Do you feel good when you DON'T have to pinch someone? What would you have done if you would have found a dead, floating fish under the boat seat?" On this, he said, "I'd have taken it easy on you and only pinched one of you. You could decide who would get the ticket." Nice guy! We didn't feel sorry for him at all when he said it would be dark when he finally portaged out of there. He had two canoes hidden along the way back into this lake. He left with an attitude that he was very disappointed that he couldn't arrest us for anything. It must have been a very productive spot for him.

Don said, "He didn't even seem to enjoy the coffee." We were just happy to see him leave. In fairness, for every warden like the last one, there seems to be a sensible one to restore your faith in the necessity for having wardens.

CHAPTER 5

HER NAME WAS QUEENIE

A Kid's Best Friend
and a Rabbit's Worst Nightmare

She was a dog from Hell on chasing out rabbits.
Where does a kid get such an unusually well-marked
and well-bred dog?

Living in Menominee, as kids, we never had any
amount of money to buy "unnecessary" things,
particularly enough extra funds to buy a quality
hunting dog. My brother and I would "walk the
bridge" over to Marinette on weekends and normally
go to a Saturday matinee.

This one Fall evening after a show, we stopped at the
Goodfellow's store. That was an unusual store for
kids to go into. It had a huge room with counters full
of a variety of cigars (I swear, there were at least 50
different varieties), etc., a back room separated by a
long curtain. I suppose so no kids or wives could see
who was at the bar. A soda counter took up a large
corner in the front room.

Not many kids went in there but if you did, it was
always with someone else. The atmosphere was
adult, and they looked a little suspicious at any kids
who came in. (Like, "Is he looking for his father?
Did his mother send him to check on someone?")

No one ever seemed to be in the front part of this store. Everyone was behind that curtain where you'd hear a lot of laughter, clinking of glasses, and it was thick with smoke.

When kids would open the front door, they would holler, "Hey!" and you'd kind of wait by the door until the bartender would stick his head out from behind the curtain and say something like, "What do you want, boys?" We'd want a malt. They made the best malts in Marinette or Menominee. After you would get your huge glass of malt (with nutmeg, no less), they'd also leave that stainless steel container for you. It was still full enough to fill your glass, another one and a half times more. As a kid, your eyes would float to the top of your head when you saw that.

After he served you, the bartender would again disappear behind that curtain where the real action was. When we finished, we'd wander around in there checking out what was 99% for the adult world. There was a cigar lighter mounted onto the counter top. It must have been a foot high, two inches in diameter, and with a pull-down handle to light it. Every kid that went in there had to pull it down, assuming that there was no adult around, to watch its huge flame.

What does all of this have to do with having a premium rabbit hound? Well, this time, when we wandered around in there, we noticed a cute Beagle pup looking at us and wagging his tail while lying near that curtain.

My brother started to pet it and it, of course, became real friendly like. We got up to go and it followed us to the door. Again, Bill got a fine idea. "If it follows us home, we couldn't help that. Maybe Mom would let us keep it." I said, "it might work." So, we pet it some more, walked a block, pet it again, and it happily followed along. We told Mom that it followed us home—right? Well, it really did. She said we could keep it unless someone claimed it. No one ever did.

We would take that dog into the slough (marsh land) near our house almost every night and he taught himself to drive (chase) rabbits in no time. This was in the 60's when there were a lot of rabbits in all of the big swamps.

When she'd bark "Rabbit," a distinctly different sound, you could usually see the one ahead of her or a "side-jumper" trying to clear out of the way. We would scatter our small party of hunters in the swamp and in a half day, we'd normally average 17-25 snowshoe rabbits. Sometime, you'd see 2-3 rabbits running in a line ahead of the dog. She would pick up extras as she ran.

We soon had a reputation of being "very good rabbit hunters," but, without our dog, Queenie, we would have been lucky to have gotten 1-2 in the same hunting time.

Jake was one of my constant hunting partners. A call to him on a Friday night to go hunting on Saturday, and he'd be standing tall by his house at 7:00 a.m. that Saturday morning. This one Saturday, his Dad wanted to go along. He had a gun, shells, and a home-made quart of tomato juice for his dinner. He said, "I've got to get away today, boys, or the wife will really get on my case," His eyes were noticeably bloodshot and a bit blurry. He didn't really look like he wanted to go hunting either, but it probably was better than facing his wife for the day as he must have really celebrated on the night before.

We drove North to a huge spruce and cedar swamp that we knew should be promising. It was just after a fresh snowfall. All tracks should be fresh and easy for the dog to flush out rabbits. We scattered out in this huge swamp. The dog was barking "Rabbit" constantly. You could hear a shot muffled from the trees and new snow over at a distance, then, a shot to your side and closer. Soon, "side-jumpers" would come hopping out slowly, feeling that they got out of the dog's way and were safe.

The ground was, of course, all covered with that new snow so all tracks were really fresh. It took two hours before I crossed one of our other hunter's tracks. Then, I noticed huge patches of what appeared to be red BLOOD wherever one of our hunter's stopped. Did someone shoot their self? I moved ahead slowly, not really wanting to see that. Then I looked closer at the blood and noticed SEEDS in it. Tomato seeds! Ed must be drinking the tomato juice and then up-chucking it soon after. I smiled and could see why he didn't want to stay home that day.

Returning from another rabbit hunt, we stopped the car to make a "nature" stop near a huge swamp. The dog naturally jumped out of the car, found a fresh rabbit track and chased it into a posted "No Hunting" area. The only way to get that dog to come back was to go and shoot the rabbit. We figured, we'd go in and out quickly and cause no problem. No luck! The landowner was in there with a hunting party and saw our dog. He confronted my brother and said, "I saw your dog chase a rabbit two times past that 'No Hunting' sign." Bill said, "The dog can't read." He explained that all we wanted to do was to catch our dog and leave. The owner reluctantly understood and we were soon on our way.

Queenie could smell out pheasants and partridge also. She wouldn't hold a point but when she was close, she would jump about three feet high as she ran forward to flush the bird. She showed no interest in chasing deer—a problem that ruined many good rabbit hunts for other hunting dogs.

We hunted with her for 17 years, then, she became blind but she still wanted to hunt. We took her out a few times and when she was barking trail, sometimes she'd hit her head full blast onto a tree trunk that she couldn't see. We had to retire her and never again had another dog quite as good as she was.

There is no greater sound to me, than hearing a rabbit hound driving rabbits in a huge swamp. The hounds run a long way away from you, then bring the rabbit back in a wide circle back to you. Sometime there are circumstances where there are also deer in the same swamp. When the dogs start barking, the deer will come crashing out to one of the hunters. It's quite a sight to see as they normally come very close to you not realizing you're also in the swamp.

You'll see a rabbit running in front of the dog, hitting the ground about every six feet on a dead run. If you're alert and quick enough, you will be having rabbit stew or HASENPFEFFER!

When the hunt is over and you close your eyes at night, it seems that you can still hear the dogs "driving rabbits" until you fall asleep.

CHAPTER 6

COON HUNTING AT NIGHT
—WITHOUT A GUN

Our camp members had never gone coon hunting in the daytime OR night. John, a full-time resident that lived near our camp, was the most experienced hunter in these local woods. He told stories of the most unusual happenings on his hunts. I'm sure most or all of them were true but to us "beginning sportsmen," they were so fantastic that they were hard to believe. He was a dead shot though. Anyone that ever saw him shoot, never questioned any stories he told about the distance, or aim of his shooting.

John came over to our camp this one Fall night and invited us to go "night coon hunting" with him. The deal was, he cut about a third of his cornfield's perimeter and left two-thirds of it standing in the middle of the field. He said, "I need at least three of you to go and it won't be dangerous. We'll use clubs on the hunt and no guns. No one needs to worry about getting shot." John never was too sure about our shooting abilities. He had two dogs that we knew would chase anything that John told them to (rabbits, coon, partridge, or head-lighters out of his fields, etc.). Three of us agreed to go on the hunt. We never heard of a hunt like this. In fact, we were really excited. Going on ANY hunt with John always meant guaranteed shooting, fast-action, and unplanned excitement. He had the only flashlight.

That's all that he wanted on the hunt. He didn't want a lot of flashing lights scaring the game away. Being in the woods at night, walking or whatever, always adds suspense, and tense imagination to a stick snapping, an animal running, and the unknown that you cannot see. This and the crisp Fall air, creates an experience one can only feel in the unpopulated country. We were tense and ready to begin.

This night had a full moon. There was enough light to see almost what you were doing. He found a club for each of us, about the size of a baseball bat. With this equipment, we started through the woods to cross a creek, then go into his field. All was going pretty well. You could see the person ahead of you well so you felt comfortable. John stopped the column to give everyone instructions. "Here's the deal," he said. "We'll cross the creek on a fallen log I know. I'll hold the light on the length of the log until you get across. Then each one of us will take positions where I show you on each side of the cornfield. We will put the dogs into the corn, and hopefully, they chase coon out to one of us and you hit it on the head with the club. It's not dangerous and if you keep real quiet, you should all see some action."

Excitedly, we started walking again and found the lot across the creek. True to his word, John held his light the length of the log so each could cross. No problem? WRONG! When I was about half way across, he was holding the light and the dogs started to bark COON!

John's reflex action, he said, immediately swung the light toward the dogs. My next step was out into open space and I fell waist deep into the creek. No sympathy from anyone. Everyone wanted to start hunting coon by that cornfield. We were placed quickly (I swear that John could see in the dark.)

I was placed on one side and my brother, Bill, was placed on an end. That was as much as I could see in the dark. The dogs were driving loudly, up and down the corn rows. If you wanted action, this was it! What was REALLY in that cornfield? Was it coon? A bear? A couple of bear? I thought, if a bear DOES come out, will I cut and run, or stand my ground and hope it runs out past me? How much courage would a person have in the dark? After all, any game had to come really close to you before you could see it. I took a good grip on that club and tried not to think about it.

One dog was driving (barking) straight towards my brother's position—and fast! I saw something run out of the field right toward him. Instead of hitting it, he jumped about two feet up into the air. It ran under him and took off into the unknown. He said that he thought it was a skunk but it turned out to be a rabbit. Score one for the coons. They ran out the other end of the field.

Then, the other dog began to drive directly toward me! I could see the cornstalks moving in a short distance. (Remember, it was dark.) Then, I could see an animal's head coming through the corn. It was low-down and it flashed through my mind that it looked big for a coon's head. I was ready. I timed my swing to the same time that it broke cover out of that cornfield, connecting full-blast on the dog's head!

It was a friendly dog. It came walking sideways toward me, its eyes rolling in its' head and its' tongue hanging out. I started to sweat and just hoped that it would recover. John said later, "That dog sure is acting funny. He must have got a whiff of something in there he didn't like." I was thinking, he sure did! After awhile, it seemed to level off. I don't think that dog ever knew or saw what hit him.

We didn't get any coon that night, but we had our share of excitement.

CHAPTER 7

WHEN PARTRIDGE HUNTING WAS PLENTIFUL

For our camp, the best partridge hunting was in the '50's and '60's. In one day's hunt (walking distance around our camp), two of us chased up about 150 partridge. Hard to believe—but true. At that time, they would fly up in coveys of 20-25.

This was in Lake Township, Menominee County. Our normal procedure for hunting them was to walk a logging road very slowly, two steps and stop and listen. Two steps and stop and listen. Keep repeating the cycle. You'd either hear one run in the dry leaves or hear one make that sucking sound that they make when they're alarmed and ready to fly.

One particular time, I had an old automatic 12 gauge shotgun and took six shells out of the car to walk a logging road about the distance of 40 acres. I didn't see any birds until I reached the end of that road. There was a small clearing on the end made by loggers as a landing. I just turned to go back when a partridge flew up. I shot it flying across the small clearing.

A second one flew up and I got it just as it was going out of sight. A third flew up and I got a clean miss. All was quiet. I put in the extra shells I had in my pocket. Figuring that was all there were, I started to walk. Two more flew up. I shot twice and got both birds. One was pretty much a cloud of feathers after I shot. Another one flew up into a tree and I shot it.

My gun was empty and I was sure that I had five birds. This was exceptional shooting for me at any time. What a good feeling! Walking out with five partridge and an empty gun.

This was some sport! We'd experiment with lighter load shells to try for better success and of course, cheaper cost with the shells. We tried #8 low-brass shot without much success in the second-growth woods. Dad said that those shells were like, "throwing a hand full of sand."

At this time period, road hunters (driving a car slowly, see a bird, stop and shoot it) were all over. Two of us were walking out of the woods to a gravel road and we saw some road hunters slowly cruising by. We thought that we'd have some fun with those guys. We took two of our partridge, pulled out the breasts to save and filled the birds up with road gravel, propped up their heads with a stick and set them along side of the road.

Almost before we were done, another car of road hunters could be heard coming. We quickly ran into the woods and waited. Soon, we heard them slam on the breaks. One guy was saying, "Hurry up, hurry up! It looks like it's going to fly!" BOOM! Someone shot and walked over to the partridge and paused there for a long while. The other guy in the car was hollering, "What's the matter?" We then heard the first hunter walk back to the car and say, "Shut up and drive." We were laughing so hard that we had tears in our eyes.

There were two times that I can remember that I got two partridge in one shot. One was standing by a stump in the woods and another was walking a half circle around it. I held off until both lined up with each other and got them both. The other time, I was walking on an old woods road that had clover about a foot high in its center. Way ahead, I saw what appeared like a partridge head. It would look up, then disappear. I shot it the next time that it showed its head. When I walked up to it, there was another one fluttering around about 10 feet directly behind it.

There were times when I'd duck hunt along small lakes in our area, see partridge walking around and never shoot them. We felt that we could always shoot partridge and didn't want to disturb the ducks. In most cases, we didn't get any ducks either.

There are so few partridge in that same area now, that we make no attempt to hunt them. Sightings now are about 2-4 birds per entire season.

We used to believe the DNR ten-year cycle explanation of poor seasons and good seasons, but not anymore. Possibly their philosophy had changed on this too by now.

There seem to be just too few of them to really bounce back to a normal hunting level.

CHAPTER 8

HAMON—AN UNFORGETTABLE CHARACTER

Everyone can remember at least one outstanding character. Mine was Hamon. He lived up on the Menominee River road and was easy to find. Although he was a small farmer, he could usually be found fishing in the river or walking in the woods. When you saw him, he'd always say he was taking a break from the farming. His breaks could last for most of the day.

One day in the '50's, I was sitting by the river, fishing at Chappee Rapids. There were no houses along there for two miles either way. After awhile, I could hear the brush cracking and the sound of something coming closer. I thought it was a deer or possibly Hamon. Then, I figured, a deer would have more sense than to be moving around at noon in the heat. I was right because here came Hamon. He was a little over five feet tall, and always wore blue bib overalls that I'm sure, were either a large or extra large size. The crotch hung down close to his knees and the side buttons were "roomy and airy" according to Hamon. He never had a pants cuff as his pants were ragged at the bottom. He said he never cut his pants off. He'd WEAR them off. He was looking up and down the river and always seemed to be looking over his shoulder for someone, like, did his wife figure out what direction he went, as she did most of the farm work. He looked my way and I waved him over. He always had a big smile and looked like he'd like to get into some mischief.

Being that it was "too hot to farm," he came down the river to cool off. He sat down with me by the river bank and checked over my fishing pole. It was propped up in a crotch of a stick with a rock holding down the handle and the line was out in the current. I was fishing walleye. Hamon was long on stories and could tell them as convincing as a minister giving his best sermon. Hamon said, "walleye, hey, this is a sturgeon hole." I knew that. Then he started, "I could tell you some fishing stories about this stretch of the river but you probably wouldn't believe me." He always baited you on, I think, to see how gullible you would be and to help add some credibility to his stories.

He leaned back with his hands behind his head and stated, "When I was younger, my brother and I would come down here at night with the boat to spear sturgeon. There were some really big ones in here then—REALLY big! We didn't have any fancy lights to use. We'd nail a pole off the front of the boat and make a wire basket to put pine knots in. When we'd light that up, it would light up the water for a good distance. One of us would stand up with the spear and the other would row the boat. If there was a sturgeon around, you could see its' eyes. They'd really shine. We'd row close to it and spear it behind the head. Now, you have to remember that these were really big sturgeon. Most people would have a rope tied to the spear and let the fish play itself out by pulling the boat around. Not us. I'd spear it, then jump on it and RIDE it around. That wooden handle on the spear made it easy to steer with. When it tired out, I'd turn it toward shore and land it. You know, a lot of people wouldn't believe that but they never saw us fish."

"The worst part, was the smoke from that burning pine pitch. It got on you and left you all black and smoky. All I could see of my brother on the walk home in the dark was his white eyeballs and teeth."

His stories beat anything you watched on T.V. in the early '50's. At this time, if you could get three "snowy" channels, you were someone looked up to in the neighborhood and you also had at least a 100 foot antenna on top of your house. I was telling him about a partridge that I had shot down where we were fishing. He said, "Well, that's where I've got you. My brother and I used to shoot a lot of partridge around here. He had a single shot 22 and I would take a burlap bag. He was really good with that 22. We'd walk slow and flush a partridge. He'd aim at it and I'd run underneath it holding that bag open. When he'd shoot, they'd drop right into the bag. Course, I could run a little faster then."

Another time, he said he noticed a rooster pheasant by his barn. He showed it to his wife from the house and said he'd go shoot it. She didn't want any part of him shooting such a beautiful bird and said she couldn't eat anything so pretty. Of course, then you ask, "Then what did you do?" He said, "I waited until it walked behind the barn where she couldn't see it. Then I went out and shot it. I pulled out the pretty tail feathers and took it into the house. I told her it was a different bird and she really enjoyed eating it."

He liked to play little jokes on strangers when he got the chance. There were 10-12 men (including Hamon) that would gather each Sunday at a neighboring bachelor's farm to play cards. There always being huge fields by the farm, a few deer would normally be standing near the field's edge most of the time. Someone had brought a pair of binoculars one Sunday (a rare item then) for the guys to see the deer. One of the regular players who came from Gladstone, brought a friend along this Sunday. Hamon took the binoculars over to the wood stove and wiped black soot around each eye piece. The eye pieces were colored black so it wasn't noticeable. He gave them to the guest and told him to check out the deer. When the fellow came back to the table, he had two black rings around his eyes like a raccoon. Everyone snickered and laughed as they played cards but didn't let on until the novelty wore off.

On another one of those famous card games (remember, this was before cable TV when a good joke was appreciated), another stranger joined the group. Hamon took him aside as soon as he arrived and told him to be very careful of his language and manners at the card table as the fellow sitting on the far right, Vic, was a minister. The stranger joined the game and was as mannerly as he could be. All of a sudden, Vic let out with an oath because of the cards he had. The visitor was petrified. Vic then gave it a few more. Hamon said the look on that visitor's face was worth losing the hand. I said, "you know, Hamon, if I didn't know you, it would be hard to believe some of this." "Ya," he said, "I know, but it's all true." Then he started to look over his shoulder again.

CHAPTER 9

A SYLVANIA EXPERIENCE

The Sylvania Wilderness Tract, hey? I had heard about it (located by Watersmeet, Michigan) but never was there. A U.P. tourist guide book claims it has 21000 acres of virgin forest. It also stressed a lot of deer, eagle, solitude, and bear.

My boys were 10 and 12 years old and wanted to go camping somewhere. Sylvania seemed like a good choice. It wasn't too far away. We could use our 14 foot boat and motor but we needed a canoe if we wanted to portage to any one of the other lakes.

I went to see my local banker (a real Goldwater conservative) for a loan on a canoe. We talked about it for awhile. He wrote down some figures for himself, looked at me over the top of his glasses and said he'd give out the loan if I left the canoe with him for collateral. I decided to check out if any of my friends had a canoe that they'd be happy to loan out for a week. We found a nice, metal, Gruman. My friend threw in a pair of car-top carriers and helped load it on. It didn't seem too heavy when the two of us loaded it.

We were trailing our 14 foot boat, had a canoe, were all loaded and the wife, two boys, and I were on our way to this wilderness area—the Sylvania Tract. After a half day's ride, we arrived at the check-in station. There, we were given a map of the chain-of-lakes, the camping sites diagram (riding in your boat, you look for a small letter nailed to a post, follow it on shore and that's the camp site), and heavy duty plastic bags to hang your food and garbage in the trees so the bear don't bother it. My wife rolled her eyes when she heard the bit about the bear. She gave me that "I don't know, Charlie," look.

Packing to stay a week here with my wife was a bit different in what I would have packed for myself (sleeping bags, cots, Coleman cooking stove, bigger tent - 7 by 7 wall tent w/frame, soap, etc.) We loaded all of this into the boat and the balance into the canoe. Then the four of us also got into the boat. It was riding noticeably low in the water. We slowly towed the canoe with our boat and went looking for the "farthest back" site. In an hour, we found it. We put up the tent while there was daylight and set up camp. It was now nearing suppertime. My wife started to make the meal (some of that dehydrated stuff where they take the moisture and flavor out of, then seal it in plastic for campers).

At this point, a forest ranger came up to our camp site. He had a boat on the shore and was carrying a short-handled shovel. He said he came to take care of the Poo. With bear on my mind, I thought, probably a small bear around here that he named "Winnie-the-Poo?" I asked him again, "take care of what?" He said, "the Poo!" Realizing, I didn't understand him, he said, "Poo, Poo, you know, the Sh-house on the hill. I came to dig a hole and clean it out." He introduced himself and seemed to want to sit and visit more than go tackle that out-house job. It also seemed that he was interested in a free meal being that it was near suppertime. He leaned over by my wife's cooking pot and asked if she was a good cook. I said, "well, I'll tell you, she sure cured that dog from begging at the table." He looked again and smelled toward the cooking pot. He got up and said he had to go one more place before dark and thought he'd do that toilet job another day.

He did want to tell us before he left, not to have any candy or sweets in the tent at night or the bear would come right in the tent after it. He no more than said that, when I saw two sets of small arms slide under the side of the tent and place two candy bars each outside of the tent. The boys were taking no chances.

The sun was now just starting to set across the water and behind a small island that was about 50 feet off shore. There was a huge spruce tree on the island with about five feet of its top cut off (probably struck by lightning). Just at sunset each night, a Great Blue Heron would land and nest there. It had about a six foot wing spread and looked beautiful in the sunset.

Being that we had a 7 by 7 wall tent, we placed two high cots against the walls and the kids in sleeping bags parallel under the cots. It looked like rain coming any minute, so we made a sizable trench around the tent. It was already pitched on the slope of a hill. As soon as we turned in, the rain started. Everything was pitch black out and the rain quickly turned into a heavy monsoon. We had lightning, heavy thunder, and water running past the tent like out of a faucet. Everyone was lying there with their eyes open. We were located among this virgin forest of 3-5 foot diameter trees. Suddenly, a tree started to crack long and steady. You knew it was going to fall. It sounded about 20 feet away and I hoped it wasn't going to fall onto the tent. After so many long seconds, it crashed onto the ground and fell about 30 feet from us. There was plenty of firewood the next day.

We fished the next morning and caught a reasonable amount of pan fish. This is the right place to bring kids for the fishing experience. The pan fish were plentiful. The boys wanted to portage with the canoe into another lake. It took all four of us to carry that heavy canoe. We must have looked like a centipede with eight legs walking under that canoe.

We got to the next lake after a lot of grunting and sweating. I thought, campers that do this regularly either have lighter canoes or are in better shape than we are. It looked like it was going to rain as soon as we got to the next lake. We agreed that we would fish a small end of the lake, trolling our fish lines. On the half-way point of the circle, a nice lake trout struck. We had him on for about five minutes. He swam by the length of the canoe like a "pass and review." (It appeared to be about 24" long.) It decided to go to the bottom and broke the line. That was the one we talked about after the trip. The big one that got away.

We got back just as the waves were picking up in size and it started to rain again. We discovered an upside down canoe gives little protection for four people. Portaging back didn't seem to take as long and we spent some quality time back in the tent.

Later in the day, when everything dried out, we packed up the 14 foot boat to find our way out to the main entrance. As things never seem to pack when you're leaving as when you came, we decided that our 12 year-old son would wait with the canoe by the campsite and I'd make a second trip to pick he and the canoe up. As a Dad, I had visions of him experiencing independence, bravery, and self-confidence by being alone while we made the first trip. When I returned, he was sitting in the canoe as far away from shore as possible with the ax across his knees, watching intently for a bear. I don't know what he learned but he seemed relieved to see me.

Anyone wanting to catch a lot of pan fish, northern, some lake trout or walleye, in a wilderness setting, I'd recommend the Sylvania Tract. It's a great place to take the kids. It's a great place to take the family.

CHAPTER 10

FISHING WITH DAD— PRECIOUS MEMORIES

This is a tribute to a Dad who taught his sons to love hunting, fishing, camping, and an appreciation for everything good about nature in the U.P.

One of the earliest experiences that I'll never forget, was when he'd take me spearing Northern Pike through the ice on the Menominee River. We had to walk about two blocks from the car to the river through deep snow to get there. He'd carry all of the equipment and half drag me behind him.

He had a tar paper fishing shack on the river that would seat four people. The fishing hole had to be cut out on each trip. This usually took about an hour to chisel out, as it was approximately two feet square on the top and normally about a foot thick. I remember, because I walked across it one time just before he was finished and crashed through to my arm pits before he grabbed me by the collar and pulled me out. He had some explaining to do on that one when we got home. I got in the house first and when the boss said, "what happened?" I told her, I think Dad tried to drown me. I thought that was a lot safer and quicker than taking the blame for showing up in frozen clothes. Things got hot for awhile but must have come out okay because he still took me or my brother on the future trips. He just would say, "be sure you sit on that damn seat!"

Winter shack ice fishing always consisted of cutting the hole, sinking newspaper to the bottom of the river (in about 10 feet of water) to brighten the hole, having a metal spear with a length of rope tied to its handle and the spearer's wrist. You'd jig a wooden fish decoy tied to a fish line tied to its balance point with the other end of the line tied to a short, wooden stick to jig up and down. The decoy had a curved tail to make it operate in circles about two feet below the ice.

We would do this for hours. Your eyes would sometimes blur, and all of a sudden, you'd see a fish swim by and soon a Northern Pike would swim slowly under the hole. You had only seconds to move the decoy to the side to keep the fish's attention on it, and work the spear without creating a splash on the surface of the water. Any one of the above could scare the fish away.

We'd usually spear 2-5 fish per trip and spend a lot of time visiting. All would be quiet and a muskrat that was swimming just below the ice could pop up with a splash in the hole. It would scare the pants off of a very young fisherman.

Other than his spearing talents, we also had some other hair raising fishing and hunting experiences. (Why is it that we always remember the weirdest and unusual events?)

Dad worked at a small, hometown dairy as a door-to-door delivery route person. He must have had the right kind of personality for the job because everyone liked him. He'd start work when most everyone else was sleeping and put in some long days. His weekends were always free though, and he was always planning some type of fishing trip. Normally, he was long on ideas and always short on preparations for the trips.

Somehow, he heard about this fantastic brook trout stream and beaver pond in the boonies near Sault Ste. Marie. At this time period (1950), a fishing trip from Menominee to the Sault area was not only a fishing trip but an adventure. Dad always gave his trips an extra twist (some of his past fishing partners always came back with excuses why they couldn't go with him on the next trip). When he'd return, though, they would come over immediately to hear about the trip. Dad liked that and like he said, "he always added a little extra color to keep their interest."

One of his best friends was half owner of the dairy so good transportation was no problem. They took one of the better dairy trucks—a Dodge panel truck. There were five of us on this particular trip (Dad and his two sons, 11 and 12 years old; his friend, Joe; and Joe's son who was 12 years old). We packed up (sparingly), and Dad only took what HE thought were necessities. I noticed that he took no blankets for himself. With the normal excitement, we started off for this God forsaken nowhere, hoping we wouldn't get lost and would catch a lot of fish. We left the main highway (I think it was highway 28), took some county roads, found some sand roads (all this from a hand-drawn map), and came to a floating bridge. When I say floating, I mean it was floating! There was high water on each side of the road and this floating bridge that looked like a wooden raft. It wasn't touching our side of the road because the high water was causing it to float free.

Now what? We all looked the situation over, jumped onto the bridge and the adults gave it a little kick. I thought that must help because I had seen adults kick car tires like that before they bought one. Dad made the decision. "We're going over. You kids go on the other side and hold the bridge to this side with your foot. I'll be coming fast. When the front wheels land on the bridge, I'm not stopping so jump out of the way."

My brother and I were positioned on the far side of the bridge. I said, "where do we jump? There's 10 feet of water right off the track of this road." He looked and rolled his eyes. Being older than me, I always felt he was wiser. He said, "When he hits the bridge, don't stop to look. Turn around and run like hell down the road." He also had longer legs than I did. The truck landed on the end of the bridge, the opposite end went up in the air and slapped back down like the sound of a huge beaver's tail on the water, and it was over . . .

Through some unknown powers, we found the beaver pond on the last sand road. It was dark when we got there. He pulled the truck off the road, half onto a foot high embankment and half on the road that was, of course, a foot lower. This left the truck floor on an inclined plane—level to sleep on. The adults didn't seem to mind because "only the kids" would sleep on the truck floor and they slept in a two-man tent. As Dad didn't take any blankets and was cold, he rolled in with us in the truck. By that time, we had already rolled onto one pile downhill. There was a lot of room on the high end of the blankets. We discovered, whoever got up to go for a "toilet call" got to sleep on the high end of the bed. Every 20 minutes, someone else would go.

At the crack of dawn, we were awakened by what seemed to be a hundred car horns. A huge flock of Canada geese were sounding off on that beaver pond. We found a really, really, old boat by the pond. Dad said, "you boys use the boat on the pond and we'll fish the stream. If the boat leaks too fast and sinks, jump out and swim for the shore." My brother smiled as he could swim like a fish. I swam like a rock. So I thought, I might just stay with the ship.

We fished worms with split shot and spinners. After awhile, we believed the only action we were going to have was bailing out that boat. The water looked black because of the muck bottom. As a fluke, we took off the sinker and cast the worm on top of the water. It slowly sank (a little faster than we were doing). Suddenly, the line started to go under in 4-6 inch jerks. We set the hook and caught some nice, fat, brookies. We fished as long as safely possible, then headed for shore to bail out more water. Dad caught smaller trout than ours on the stream. When he saw ours, he said, "I figured I put you guys in the best spot." Actually, we thought he was surprised to see us still floating.

As we were driving home, he was smiling and while looking out the truck window said, "Wait until you guys hear about the next trip I've got in mind." The more remote they were, the more he loved it. I was thinking, what would top that floating bridge and that leaky boat?

CHAPTER 11

THE FIRST DEER HUNT WITH DAD— PRECIOUS MEMORIES

Dad started into deer hunting late in life so he was really a beginner like my brother and I. We were hunting on opening day of our first season. When we were walking back to the camp at noon, Dad said, "we'll make a deer drive. You post on the end and I'll drive to you." I didn't know anymore about this than he did but figured, a 40-acre drive, one driver and one poster on the end of the drive, with no other hunters posting on the sides didn't seem like a good plan. Unbelievably, a small spike-horn buck came out to me. I took a shot at its head and stunned it. It fell, got up, put its head down and charged me like a bull (so I thought). Later, I reasoned, it was running on a well-used trail that I was standing on.

There was a frozen pond in front of me and I was standing against a big tree. It hit the pond on a flat-out run and I shot it again. It then skidded across the pond and would have hit me had I not jumped out of the way. Dad came through, saw the deer, but felt the three-inch spikes (exactly) weren't legal. I tagged it but he said we'd better take it to camp after supper because he wasn't sure. After supper, it was REALLY dark. In fact, it was pitch black!

We found our way back to the deer as we could follow our tracks in the snow. Dragging it out along the side of a field was no problem until we came to a barbed wire fence bordering the road. The deer's legs had rigor mortis. We lifted it half way through the fence and it wouldn't go any farther. One leg was tangled with a strand of wire and another leg was tangled with another wire. We'd push and the wire would screech loudly. When we pulled, it would screech an octave higher. Dad was an excitable person. The more we pushed and pulled, the more excited he got. It struck me so funny to see him so excited, I laughed until I had to sit down. Then to add a new dimension, car headlights started to come over the hill. We pushed, pulled, laughed, and didn't get anywhere. The car finally turned off to another road and we relaxed and lifted the wire from the deer legs and slid it through.

Another time, we (Dad, brother and I) were walking in at noon hour and we saw a buck and a doe run behind two pine trees, then step out of view. Dad said, "We'll all line up on that first tree (that's where he said the buck was) and shoot through the tree." We did. Each one of us put two rounds through that tree. The buck ran out undisturbed. We never touched him. We watched him run away as we didn't believe we could hit a running target. We probably were right.

The next year, he was hunting with a long-barreled 32 Special. He was 6'2". When he set that gun on the ground and held it upright, it seemed to be about a foot shorter than him. He came back to camp one day all excited and kept saying, "I saw a buck with lots of horns and ears as big as paddles." The buck was laying on the side of a ridge and it moved its ears back and forth when it saw him. He claimed he couldn't see the end sight of that long barrel and didn't get a shot. Buck Fever?

He later became one of the best hunters that I ever hunted with. In his later years, I'd pick him up on weekends to go to the camp. If I was 15 minutes late, he'd be sitting on a chair in his driveway waiting and say, "what took you so long?"

Last year, he broke his hip and had to move into a nursing home. We visited him every day possible and talked over fishing and hunting experiences. Then, time took its toll. About two weeks before he went to a happier hunting grounds, he took my hand, looked me in the eye and said, "I love you." I always felt that way toward him but can't remember either one of us ever saying that to one another.

If there's a heaven, I'm sure he's got a good deer post on a good trail or is probably playing Schafskopf (Sheep Head) with St. Peter.

Precious memories? They were ALL precious memories.

CHAPTER 12

FRED—ANOTHER
UNFORGETTABLE CHARACTER

For Fred, life was meant to be an adventure. As soon as he was finished with his eight-hour job, he'd have a smile from ear to ear and was planning something BIG! If he liked it, he'd do it three times as much as the normal person. Fred had 13 kids.

Fred had a philosophy that the Lord put all those game animals and fish on the earth to feed somebody. There was no reason why his kids couldn't survive on them. He would hunt and fish with a passion. He, for some reason, thrived on work. There was no stopping him once he started a project. He'd work all day and through the night at it, or until he ran out of beer. He'd say, "There's no stopping me now boys. Beer is like a lubricant to 'oil you up.'"

The neighborhood kids loved to hang around his house and wait for him to start some bold and sometime, weird project. He loved rabbit hunting and his kids ate those rabbits with a passion. When I think of it, they ate everything with a passion. Fred couldn't get those rabbits fast enough. He decided to raise a few tame ones in his backyard. He started out with four and they really multiplied.

His rabbits did two things well, they'd eat and breed, eat and breed. Fred said, "Look at them go! Just like perpetual motion." Then, he'd proudly say, "I think it runs in the family." Well, those rabbits kept reproducing and Fred kept building more rabbit coops. Pretty soon, he had one very long and high column of rabbits and coops stacked on top of each other on one side of his yard.

All was well until his drinking partner, Rab, came over. They started to "unwind" as Fred would put it. Then Rab discovered the rabbits in the backyard. He dumped out their water dishes and filled them all up with beer. Those rabbits LOVED it! They'd drink some, run around their small coops as fast as they could, drink some more and then kick their hind legs hard in the air. Of course, Rab then had to put some of the bucks in with the doe rabbits. They seemed to have a ball! Drink—run around—mate, drink—run around—mate.

Rab said, "Watch this boys. Here's a sex education lesson for you. He watched and thought for awhile, then said, "Just don't go at it so fast."

Another time, Fred wanted to go perch fishing in Green Bay but couldn't buy any minnows. He had his own minnow net so he and his friend, Rab, got into his pickup truck to go seine minnows Some of us kids got into the back end figuring this too could develop into something. His net was about 40 feet long. Fred held one end and Rab held the other. Fred had no boots so the depth of the water meant nothing to him. He got into the water as far as the net would stretch and Rab stayed on the shore. Fred gradually went out farther and farther. First, the water was up to his knees, then his waist. He spotted a swarm of minnows in the net, smiled from ear to ear and said he was going deeper.

Pretty soon, he was up to his neck pulling the net with him. Rab hollered to him, "If you plan on going over your head, hang onto the net. We don't want to lose the minnows." Fred must have realized how deep it was then because he circled to the shore. He used whatever minnows he caught: chub, sucker, or perch. "They all catch fish," he said.

Fred's Garage. He was a fair carpenter. One year, he decided, he and Rab would build a huge garage in his back yard. Room for projects and the car. Rab asked him questions continually when they were building, like, "How many nails are you putting in each board." How many boards will it take to cover one side, etc. etc.?" Then Rab started on one end of the roof and Fred on the other putting roofing shingles on. After awhile, Rab said, "What do we do when we meet in the middle?" Fred, without blinking an eye, said, "We'll kiss!" That ended all of the questions.

Fred's New Shotgun. It was a nice pump action 20 gauge. We noticed right away that the serial numbers were all filed off before he got it and asked him what happened to them? "You don't need them on there boys, don't need them at all. They don't make it shoot straighter. They're just some such numbers for the factory's use." We all knew right there, Fred got a real deal on that gun.

One other day, about six of us were at his house and he said, "boys, I need your help." We need to move that freezer from the downstairs entrance to an upstairs bedroom." We never questioned Fred. His answers would leave you just as confused so we all got a hold of that freezer and started upstairs. It was about the length of a coffin and felt like it could have been holding a small deer herd stacked neatly in there. We inched it upstairs and finally into a bedroom. Just what every bedroom needed. Later, we heard Fred got a scare of a game warden checking certain freezers. No game warden in his right mind would have thought normal people would have taken that monster of a freezer up all of those stairs.

I mentioned before, he did everything on a big scale. One of his real biggies was during smelt season. This one particular year, he found a farm hay conveyer and remade it to load smelt from a creek into the back of a truck. One night, he set it all up and after a few beers, was ready for business. Of course, the conveyer wasn't designed for this so when they'd dip the smelt onto the conveyer, a good share would fall off on the way up to the truck. Soon, the creek bank was white with spilled smelt. Fred didn't mind because they were really running and plentiful. Soon, he or a friend would struggle up that slippery, smelt-covered bank to get a beer from the truck. They then would fall back into the creek when trying to return down that slippery bank. The lucky ones later just slid down on their rears like down a kid's slippery slide. All you could hear was Fred saying, "More beer, more smelt, more beer, more smelt."

Then, with one eye open and watching the road intently, they managed to bring that load to his garage to begin cleaning them. I'll say this for Fred. He was one persistent soul! They drank and cleaned fish all through that night. I don't believe he threw any away. He just smiled the next morning and said, "My baby dolls really like these fish." His kids looked back at him like they were going to up-chuck. They already had their fill of those fish. Fred said, "Yes, sir, the land of the plenty. The baby dolls really love these fish. Pass me another beer, Rab." We couldn't have seen a more exciting show than this on TV.

Making Homemade Wine. His oldest son attempted to make a HUGE batch of homemade wine (a famous first!). He put apples, yeast, raisins, sugar, rhubarb (for an extra kick) and water together. That stuff started to ferment and boil until it formed a "rolling boil" from the chemical action of these ingredients. It was in the basement for two weeks before Fred discovered it. He said his son came up one day kind of walking sideways and smiling. "I knew right off, that there was something wrong with the boy."

He said, his friend, Rab, came over and volunteered to get rid of the batch for him. Rab went downstairs and later came up kind of "hollow-eyed." Fred asked him if he got rid of it. Rab said, "Yaaa. After you got past the raisins it wasn't all that bad."

Watching the Stock Car Races. Spies Field, in Menominee, was developed as a stock car track for some years. There was sand dumped along the cement walls of the field from top to bottom. This was to prevent injury to the drivers if they would "spin out." Once in awhile, a tire or other car part would come off and roll up that inclined plane of sand, right over the top of the wall and into the surrounding woods.

Fred figured out a system to beat the price of tickets for all of us. He had a very long and strong wooden plank and two higher than normal ladders (everything Fred had was higher than normal). Two or three kids would carry a ladder and about three kids would carry the plank. Fred would walk ahead to find a choice spot to set up this "scaffold" of a plank between the two ladders for our seat just outside the cement wall. We sat about waist high from the top of this wall. He picked the most dangerous corner of the track because "we want to see the action." Once, a tire came off of a car and came hell bent up the sand

right at us. Fred shouted, "Bend down for the tire!"
We all bent down below the wall and that thing
whistled over our heads and crashed into the woods
behind us.

He looked at us and said, "Don't worry, boys, the
Lord's on our side." I thought, Ya the Lord and that
damned tire!

CHAPTER 13

RABBIT HUNTING NEAR FELCH— IN THE ITALIAN CAMP

We drove up to the Big Buck camp from Iron Mountain to hunt rabbits. It was a Saturday and EARLY. As my Father-in-law put it, "This bunch doesn't like to waste any part of a weekend." It was about 5:30 a.m., cold, and as far as I was concerned, sleeping time. The Father-in-law said, "We'll probably be the last ones to get there. Tell them we had problems with one of the dogs rather than that you overslept." He was always proud of being on time and one of the early ones.

Those hounds were something else. Two blue ticks that stood just past your knees, they always seemed hungry and had about the most stinky breath that I ever smelled when they'd lean their big heads over to the front seat.

After about an hour and a half drive (there was a lot of snow) we could see the single lane road going into the camp. The Big Buck Camp! They could have just as well have called it the Italian Camp. There were eight owners and all were 100% Italian, my Father-in-law included.

The road into camp was plowed out well. This was impressive as there was about two feet of snow on the level and the road in was the distance of 40 acres.

Soon, we sighted the camp. The parking area was also plowed out as good as any shopping center. There was three cars there already.

Smoke was coming out of the chimney and some of the guys were looking out the window to see who was coming. They were all smiles. Good friends, a full weekend at camp, plenty of beer and food and a rabbit hunt. They had to tell us how Penny (they all have nicknames), parked out by the main road and waited for the county plow to come by. When it did, he waved them down, pointed to their camp road and held up two six-packs of beer. Penny said, "I could see that I had their attention but they said they couldn't plow private roads, especially not until the highways were done."

Then, Penny said, "I held up a whole case of beer. Their tongues were licking their lips and the driver finally nodded his head." "Yes." Vompa said, "Hell, we could hold a dance up here with this nice, plowed lot."

You could smell the bacon frying as they were just making breakfast. I was thinking, we got here late? We're just on time. My Father-in-law liked to cook. That was one of his main hobbies. I figured he'd still make the "big meal." He brought up a huge container of homemade spaghetti sauce that he cooked the entire previous night, homemade meatballs, spaghetti, hand-grated cheese, and Schinderele's Italian Garlic Bread that he always added a "little extra" garlic too. This, with Italian red wine that was already at camp, was a real feast, especially after hunting in the cold for about four hours.

There were a total of 14 guys at the camp. There were enough double beds to sleep six. They had a system for this and everyone seemed to take it as routine. They'd play cards all night. Some would sleep while some played cards. After so many hours, they'd wake up the sleepers and change places. All I can remember about the sleeping was that from the cold air outside, hunting, red wine, and getting up so early, I slept like a baby. I do remember that the sheets were pretty sandy down by our feet.

The basement of the camp was one huge dug-out cellar. I swear, it must have been held up with beer cases. One of the members was a U.P. beer distributor and as the other's put it, it was his solemn duty to keep the cellar filled with cases of beer.

The camp had two excellent cooks. My Father-in-law, Smudger, was one and Nardi was the other. I don't think there is a supper club in the whole U.P. (and we've got some good ones) that has better taste or quality food compared to these two. It was interesting. Whenever these two took turns cooking, everyone would rave about the quality of the meal, except the other cook. They never complimented each other. I think they both thought there could only be one #1 cook and that was himself.

There always seemed to be pancake batter on the back of the stove, a big pan of cut-up rabbit in "red sauce" and polenta. Whoever came in at any time could make themselves a meal. Some always came in early and would be playing cards. They always had reasons why they came in early. "Penny got cold so I had to come in with him, or the damn dogs weren't driving too good. Must be too cold for their nose to smell any tracks." The hunt seemed secondary to the camp life.

The hunt. They had four dogs, two blue ticks and two beagles. The hunters split into two groups. One half started on one end of the swamp with two dogs and the other half did the same on the remaining half of the swamp. The plan was that the dogs would chase up more rabbits and they'd provide shooting for each group as the rabbits would run the whole swamp.

The snow was so deep that the rabbit runways were deep trenches in the snow. They were actually hard to see under the thick cedar in those sunken runways. One of the most pleasant sounds is hearing good hunting dogs driving rabbits in a thick swamp. The sound is sometime muffled by the dense trees, then very loud through small clearings or when the dog sights the rabbit and becomes extra excited.

Those two blue ticks had a mournful sound like hearing bloodhounds chasing an escaped prisoner in a southern movie. The beagles were good hunters but had trouble breaking through the snow with their shorter legs. What they lost by this, seemed to be made up with a strong heart and a love for their work.

One of those beagles was driving a rabbit my way (the dog on a chase doesn't bark all the time), and I suddenly saw the flash of white coming down one of those sunken trails. I shot and a second later, saw it was the white tail of the dog and not a white snowshoe rabbit. His tail was going back and forth like a windshield wiper when I shot. I must have shot to the right when he wagged left because he wasn't hurt. We shot 26 snowshoe rabbits that day.

My Father-in-law came through the swamp to meet me and said, "Aren't you getting cold? We could go in, warm up and play some cards." It seemed like, you needed an excuse to go in and it was more macho for him if I was cold. I said, "Sounds like a good idea." I knew I was "saving face" for him and hey, that rabbit in red sauce and polenta looked pretty good!

CHAPTER 14

THOSE HUNTER'S BALLS (DANCES)

Every deer season, the taverns large enough to hold a dance in our area, would sponsor a Hunter's Ball.

To a couple of single guys, at that time, it meant a chance at a new rifle on a raffle, good music, a lot of lies told by those hunters that successfully shot a deer, beer, and GIRLS.

My brother was the best "date-getter" from our crowd at these dances. He'd say, "There's nothing to it guys. They want us as much as we want them. The trick is to find out which ones."

This one time, John, a camp member, and Jim were having a beer at the bar. John appeared more than ready to dance with some lucky girl he spotted. As the single girls were normally always in groups of twos, he wanted Jim to hurry up and go dance with the other one. Jim said, "After three more beers." John looked around in desperation and called the bartender over. He took out his wallet, and said, "Give him three more beers." Jim drank them, one, two, and three and went to dance. I felt sorry for some of those girls. They got a date all right but they also got some rather rough dancing along the way.

Dad would say before we would leave for the dance, "You young guys, remember, you have to be in good shape to be on your posts before light tomorrow." We all promised that we would. We figured that we could sleep on the post as well as in the camp. And that fresh air had a way of putting you to sleep out there. We'd doze, wake up, and nod off again. There were times that we hoped we wouldn't see a deer.

We returned to camp after this one venture, got out of the car, and Bill said, "We don't sing too well, guys, but we sure do sing LOUD!"

That night, we woke up and couldn't find Jim in the camp. He came about half way to the camp and went to sleep under an evergreen tree. When we brought him in, he said, "Don't worry guys, the deer sleep like that every night."

Many of those Hunter's Balls were a "one time a year" visit for members of distant camps. They gave the deer season a festive mood of a second New Year's Eve.

CHAPTER 15

OUR SECOND DEER CAMP

About half of the hunting camps in our area of Menominee County were always truly family camps. This was one of them. That's where the feeling of a traditional family gathering came about at our camp.

We'd take our vacations for this time. My brother closes his barber shop for the first days. He places that old buck head-mount in the barber chair with a sign, "Gone Hunting" when he leaves. It's so traditional that it reminds you of a Norman Rockwell painting.

This camp has a huge wood/coal Heatrola for its heat source. Like any wood stove, it's either too cold or too hot in camp. It heats the place up quickly but then, doesn't know when to quit and the temperature keeps going up.

As hot as it is in the evening, it can be just the opposite in the morning. Everyone tries to out wait the next one to get up and make the fire.

This is a true hunting camp. It has the survival necessities and a lot of stories and good spirit to last a lifetime.

The most unusual shot story has been Bill's. He was posted on opening day on the highest ridge we have. It overlooks a cedar swamp and behind that, a long, narrow lake. Along about 8:30 a.m., he saw a good size buck swim across the lake towards him. He couldn't tell how many points but said it looked respectful with a high rack. He could actually see it most of the time moving through the cedar swamp because he was up so high.

That deer came out as if it was planned to be right in front of him and stood broad side. He said it was about a 100 yard shot and downhill. He took a resting aim on a tree limb, aimed for the front shoulder and squeezed off a shot from his 300 Savage.

The buck flinched and kind of "walked on its tiptoes back into the swamp." He found it standing or maybe leaning against a tree just looking at him. He walked up closer and shot it again. It dropped on the spot. Why did the buck act so odd after the first shot? Bill's first shot clipped its testicles clean off. That buck was one humble bumble.

This camp had one of our best deer posts. The shed window—talk about comfort! The post was always dry, out of the wind, a comfortable chair, bait pile, and a four-sectioned window with one section missing. We would shoot through the fourth missing section.

If it was a slow day and no deer were coming to this post, you could sit back and listen to the mice running all around in there and hope that they didn't run on you.

One wet day, during bow and arrow season, Ben said he'd use that post. At the least, he'd be dry. After awhile, a nice five-point buck came into the bait pile. Ben said, he eased the bow back but then had to wait because the deer's rear was facing him. Ben had a problem with waiting to long because then he'd get buck fever and shake all over.

He said that he waited until it turned, pulled back the bow some more, took a fine aim and KER-THUNK! His arrow shot the middle wood frame of the window dead center. No one but no one could top that story for a few years.

Visiting the other deer camps at night seems to be a required ritual. Everyone wants to see what the next camp has shot, hear their stories, some true, some lies, like ours, and drink a little beer. (More detail in the next chapter.)

CHAPTER 16

VISITING THE OTHER DEER CAMPS AT NIGHT—A RITUAL

The first day or two of the deer rifle season, all of the camps in our area stay pretty much to themselves. They hope they don't get any company until they have built up some "bragging rights" on the buck pole.

About the third day, as soon as it gets too dark to hunt and the camp members have eaten supper at their own camps, the ritual begins, to visit the other camps. Why do we eat first at our own camp? I've seen some weird things cooked up in some of the other camps. One guy was frying up a huge woodpecker one year when we came in. He looked normal when he was doing it. He said something like, "That damn woodpecker isn't going to knock on his post anymore."

You never know what you are eating and they are offended if you don't eat with them. Other than that, these good ole boys buy better groceries for camp than they eat at home (whole beef tenderloins, steaks, hickory-smoked hams, and as one hunter said it, bacon that's a whopping $3.00 a pound and 20 miles out of the way to go get it.

But, after all, deer season is a very special vacation for most every hunter. The beer and "fully-stocked" bars, and as Ben say's, "Flow's like kid's candy, or

Trick or Treating on Halloween." It's an unusual camp that doesn't offer a courtesy drink. For more, you have to patiently wait out the story telling of their hunt, then they gladly keep it flowing.

Ben knew of one camp that he was suspicious of always eating "premature" venison (shot before season). Last year, we stopped there. They have a long road in (about 20 acres from the last gravel road). We set our six-volt light with the red side flashing lenses on our windshield and drove slowly in. We stopped about 200 yards from the camp. Suddenly, the camp lights went off and that was the quietest camp I ever have seen. When we finally were invited in, I didn't see or smell any cooking. The camp owner just said, "Just a force of habit, boys. We were thinking of going to bed."

Everyone always checks to see if there is a rookie or a "city" Lower Michigan hunter in the camp. If so, you can expect someone to tell a "true" story about, normally, the huge black bear that they discovered sleeping in the outhouse. This was a good story particularly when it would be pitch black outside and after a few drinks when the fellow "had the urge." He'd look longingly at the outhouse and no one wanted to go out there with him.

At my friend, Gene's, camp, he'd brag that his wife never comes up to the camp during season. "We have a deal. I never go home either." One guy asked, "How many more days did you say you'd be up here, Gene?"

These trips are also hunting skill exchange times. Someone did something different this year to hunt that worked and we'll pass it on to whoever would like to try it. The sharing, good conversation, and friendships that develop from this seem to form a common bond that lasts throughout the year.

CHAPTER 17

OUTDOOR SPORTS *CAN* AFFECT YOUR EDUCATION
Or—You Can't Fool Dad

My parents always had a high regard for doing well in school. They both did well as "natural students" but grew up in the Depression and it wasn't in the cards for them to go past high school.

I was a comfortable "C" student. I didn't have to strain myself to get a C. Therefore, I got C's. The teachers would only call on you once during a period. They were satisfied because you weren't failing and would zero in on someone else. Your parent's felt you were in the safe zone too, and weren't really sure of anything else. I'd sit in class and dream of hunting, trapping, or fishing.

One day, a high school vocational teacher approached me and said that two study halls were too much for me. I should take a vocational program where I could be excused from one study hall, work in a job training site and receive school credit for it.

I thought about that and decided it was a fine idea. I talked to the owner of a small dairy where I worked on weekends to sign for me so I could be excused two hours early from school for work. He said he didn't have employment for only two hours. I talked him into signing me out for employment anyway and I went hunting two hours early. Life couldn't have been better. The teacher was really excited. He kept telling me I was in an innovative, new, program of learning. I thought this high school curriculum was good! All you had to do was be flexible and look for the weak spots.

Then, before the next deer season, I made a very miscalculated mistake. Dad always went to deer camp for a full week. I asked him if I would raise all of my grades on the next report card to A's and B's, would he allow me to go hunting for the full week, too? He thought it over for awhile, I suppose, figuring that it was a safe bet because I never rose much higher than a C except in Physical Education. So, he agreed. To make this short, I worked hard at it and got all A's and B's.

I heard he and my mother talking it over one night after report cards came out. I think they were more flabbergasted than they were proud of those grades. Dad said, "Sure, I could go to the deer camp for a week." I felt things couldn't GET any better! There really IS a God!

When we got home from "a week up North," he had a heart-to-heart talk with me about school, grades, and how things were GOING to be. He didn't leave any room to wiggle about not getting good grades. If you could do it once, you could do it forever!

I'm sure that he knew about the "cooperative vocational work agreement" with the dairy. He probably thought that he'd leave me something. Life changed and I learned. I also learned that I couldn't fool Dad.

CHAPTER 18

ANDY—ANOTHER
UNFORGETTABLE CHARACTER

Andy lived in a log cabin with his bachelor brother across the road, and then down some, from our camp. Their cabin was really, really old but they had something that we didn't have. They had an outside, hand, water pump with excellent water.

When we bought our camp, it didn't have any water at all. We'd go over and fill our water containers at Andy's and naturally, had to go inside for a visit. One reason, it was the thing to do when you received something from someone else. Another, opening their cabin door was like going into a mystic adventure. It was a different world.

How those two guys survived in that cabin year after year should have qualified them for some kind of medal (if they were in the service). The water pump was about 50 feet from the cabin. When we'd pump water there in the winter, you could actually see "lines of light" on the snow at night created from the light inside the cabin reflecting outside through the cracks between the upright log sides of the cabin.

When you opened the door, the first thing you noticed were the two, bare, light bulbs glowing brightly. The second thing was a wood heater in the center of the room sizzling and burning noisily like it was having a hard time keeping itself warm. Andy only burned "green" wood. He didn't believe in having a seasoned wood pile on hand. Each day, he'd go out and cut a few, necessary trees to survive until the next day. On a cold, below-zero morning, you could hear him cutting trees with his ax (ca-chink, ca-chink) and Fin saw. Just enough.

The other furnishings were a long sofa, kitchen table and chairs, and a few extra wood chairs. There was also an old organ taking up one whole corner of the building. He said, "The organ don't work. Some day, I might get it fixed." I couldn't imagine why. I think if they would have moved it out of the building, it may have off-set the balance of that old cabin and caused it to tilt.

There were two piles (always) of magazines stacked about three feet high on each end of the sofa. When you'd come into the cabin, Andy would normally be leaning over the wood Heatrola, "keeping warm." I don't think they put on any more clothes to go outside than they did to survive inside. Periodically, like once a year, we'd notice two social workers visit there. They'd stay for about an hour, take pictures of the cabin from the outside (probably the inside too), and then leave. Andy seemed to tolerate them because about a week after the visit, a load of coal would be delivered and dumped off in their yard from the city.

Andy did all of the cooking and baking. When he baked in the winter, the smell of that fresh bread was overpowering as you stepped in. Unfortunately, keeping things clean was not one of their important virtues.

This one time, one of our camp members, Gene, visited them. The fresh bread was just put on the back counter and was cooling. Gene said, his mouth was watering for some but he was understandably a little leery of it. Andy cut him a slice and placed the butter on the table for him. He told him that it was really, really, good. Especially that caraway seed they had in it. Andy looked over casually to his brother and said, "Those mice must have gotten into the flour again." They were good guys but by most people's standards, not the cleanest.

To sit down there, you had to first clean off something to sit on. I cleared off a spot on the sofa and sat down. After I was sitting there for about five minutes, Andy said, "Maybe you better not sit on that." My eyes started to flash around and I said, "Why? Snakes?" He said the sofa was pretty full of mice. It was good enough for him but he said it seemed to bother the company. His brother said, "Yeah, there's a pine snake that comes in under the door, goes across the kitchen floor and out a hole on the far wall. I'm going to have to catch it one of these days."

If anything ever bothered Andy, he never let it show. Once a month, things probably "built up" in him and he'd go to the closest tavern and "hang one on." He ran short of cash and couldn't pay his bar bill so the tavern owner let him bring in so many cedar posts to pay for his booze. The bar owner would brag about how he would "short" Andy on the value of the cedar that he brought in. Andy, later heard about this and told someone, "The jokes on him because I'm not cutting that cedar on MY land." There was an 80-acre parcel of land belonging to a party from Chicago behind Andy's that they would pay taxes on but never came from Chicago to use it. Andy felt that it was "open range."

Some weeks the brothers shaved and some weeks they didn't. When we'd leave, Dad said, "You know, they always say, bachelors got it made compared to getting married. I go over and see those guys and really am grateful to go home to clean sheets and good cooking."

Dad always had a way to smooth out an odd situation. He'd say, "Don't worry about those guys, boys. They never get sick. A germ couldn't live on either one of them."

CHAPTER 19

MY FIRST BOAT AND MOTOR—A CURSE?

When you can't afford something and you're a Yooper, you make one. That idea built my first boat. Jim, my best friend, came up with the idea. I said, "Neither one of us ever made a boat." He thought about that for a second and commented, "What makes you think we can't?"

So, two high school seniors began casually, measuring parts of boats that we thought we could copy. We agreed that we'd make it in our basement so it had to fit through the door and the stairway. The house had a straight stairway (no turns) so the basement was blessed with a winter project.

The boat was made of plywood. Having no "boat mold forms," we used ropes to bend in the bow against wooden side braces. It would be a flat-bottomed, 12 footer. Good for river fishing and perch fishing on Green Bay for anyone who liked to live dangerously.

We had a zillion chrome screws to screw it together as Jim's dad worked at a furniture factory and screws were plentiful. My dad was a big help. He'd come downstairs and ask, "Are you using waterproof plywood?" We'd say, "Sure, Sure." Another time, he checked it over and said, "Are you using waterproof glue?" "Sure, Sure. Oh ya." Towards the end, when it was shaping up, he'd come down and measure the boat and remeasure the door and stairway. I don't think he had all that much confidence in our measurements. (After all, he saw our math grades from school.)

At that time, everyone else in the high school woodworking class was cutting out end tables that the teacher said, "Your mother's will really appreciate this at Christmas." We were cutting out boat ribs and seats for a project the instructor never saw. I suppose he felt that at least they're constructively busy.

After a coat of paint, it looked pretty sharp, and that boat was built strong! We had screws spaced every inch along its bottom. You could have dropped it from the top of the car and I'm sure nothing would break.

The motor was a three horsepower—Ward's Sea King. It had to be the toughest product that Wards ever sold! It went through hell and back with us. The gas tank was located inside the motor cover (no side tank with connecting hose). To fill the tank after the motor was running hot for a few hours was a dare rather than routine.

As you probably know, most motors won't start after they are "flooded" with gas. This one had character. To start it, you always had to flood it until a few drops of gas appeared on the water. Then, pull the starter cord and it would sound like an airplane engine. It trolled perfectly slow and made a lot of noise. There was no slip-clutch on it so it routinely broke propeller shear pins.

Fishing Walleye on the Menominee River by Old Rock "Cribs." We were trolling for walleye by Chappee Rapids one evening, staying close to old "rock cribs" placed periodically as barriers during the early logging days. We picked up a few nice ones and because of the dark, ran the propeller into the rocks. We used anything for a shear pin that would work. This particular trip, we were using a cut-off nail. The nail (being stronger than a shear pin was supposed to be) didn't break and the motor kept running until it forced itself to stop. We took the motor home and had a bent and jammed drive shaft. I took it apart, rolled the shaft around on the cement sidewalk and pounded it straight with a hammer. It worked as good as new!

Perch fishing on Green Bay was a real challenge with this boat. One, you had to wait for a calm-water day to go onto the bay in this flat-bottom boat, and two, you had to keep an eye on the weather conditions to go in fast if the water got rough.

This particular day, the weather and water were both calm. My partner and I started out fishing along a commercial fisherman's "lead-net" until we came to his round "pond" net. Normally, perch would follow this route and one would have good fishing luck. When conditions were calm, nothing would bite. Then, as the water began to get choppy, the perch started to bite. The water gradually became rougher and the fishing success increased. WE STAYED TOO LONG! Suddenly, there was a quick change in the weather and the waves turned into 10 foot droughts and waves. We were about a half mile from shore and I had an odd feeling that our number may be up. There isn't much high speed with a three-horsepower motor.

When our boat went down into a drought, you couldn't see anything but water around you. When it came up to the crest of a wave, the motor's propeller would come out of the water completely, roar loudly, and the boat would start turning in a different direction. My brother grabbed the oars and jammed them into the water when we hit the top of a wave to hold the boat straight. We had no control whatever, to go across the waves into shore or we would have filled the boat with water. I had to steer the boat into the wave direction. We checked our survival options quickly. We had a half full gas can that we figured would float if we could hold onto it, and we agreed to hang onto the boat. No one had life jackets at this time.

After about an hour of being at the mercy of the waves, we hit the shore. The next wave coming in, completely filled our boat with water. We landed a good three miles from where we started out and had left the car. I don't think we said ten words all the way home. We both knew that we were close to the Pearly Gates.

Fishing off of Henes Park in Menominee another time was also a lasting experience. The fishing was good, so we came back in late, after dark. We had done this periodically, before, so we didn't think much about it. After getting a directional bearing from the lights along the shore, this night, we cut in too short around the park's rocky point and the motor stopped. I looked back in the dark and to my shock, saw no motor and the top half of the boat's transom (boat's back) was missing. We had a safety chain attached so I slowly pulled it back in. Nothing. The chain had broken in half. Anchoring the boat quickly and searching with a flashlight, we saw a blue streak from the motor in 20 feet of water. Bill lit up a railroad flare that we carried in our fishing box and stuck it into the front of the boat for light. Unknown to us, cars were now stopping on the point in Henes Park and wondering what happened. I took off my clothes, went over the side and followed the anchor rope down. Feeling the motor with my feet, I picked it up and brought it to the surface following the anchor rope. We got it alongside the boat and it became a struggle to boost it back in and at the same time, keep the rear of the boat high enough in the water so water didn't come in over the missing half of the boat's transom.

We noticed the shore-people then. They were shouting, "Do you need help?" Did he drown? Should we call the Fire Department?" We quickly put out the railroad flare so we didn't attract more attention and hollered back, "Everything's okay." I don't think anyone heard us because I could hear, "I think they went under!"

We couldn't row toward them because of the rocks so we rowed around the park and to our car. The crowd finally broke up and we didn't hear any fire trucks.

Fishing the Menominee River again for walleye near what's called the Oxbow. There are no homes in this area, only hunting camps and this was fishing season. My brother and I were trolling with that same motor and it ran out of gas. Ka-put, it stopped. We were in very deep water with a good current.

I opened the gas tank cap and poured in some gas and spilled some also, over the motor. On the first pull of the starter cord, the surplus gas ignited! You could only see the motor handle sticking out. The rest of the motor was a ball of flames!! I unscrewed the motor clamps and dunked the motor into the river. Holy Wah! The Lord must have been smiling on us that day. No one got hurt as it could have exploded at any second.

We beached the boat and Bill started the mile walk up-river to get the car and trailer. I dumped out the gas and cleaned the motor's spark plugs, and refilled it with fresh gas, gave it a few pulls and it started! I picked Bill up about halfway to the car. That was one tough motor. Bill still has it yet today. He said he doesn't use it. He just likes to look at it and remember our fishing experiences. He said, "Strangers wouldn't believe what we did with that motor."

CHAPTER 20

THE CROSS-EYED BUCK
(Parts of this story are absolutely true!)

We first saw it in early November last year, rubbing its head on a tree, or so we thought. Later, we discovered, it was going down a runway and side-stepped into that tree. There was something definitely wrong with that buck; double-vision, cross-eyed, or both. He had a rack that extended about 24" wide with two points straight up from his head and three points on each side, way out on the ends.

Our camp yard has about three acres of cut lawn. We throw apples and corn out there just to watch the deer. This is an understood, "no hunting" area. It may seem strange but we walk a mile into the woods to hunt but whatever deer came onto the lawn, we enjoy watching and don't shoot them. I think that started because they are mostly does. Now, the cross-eyed buck might be something else! When he looks at you, he doesn't look right. He looks like "he's got one oar out of the water," "one brick short of a load," or "not playing with a full deck."

He came into the camp yard one day to eat apples. He'd always bite twice; once where he thought the apple was and once where it actually was. He'd do this real fast, chomp! chomp!—because it was routine for him.

We learned from watching him, that he'd do most everything twice and fast! I suspect because of his vision. Last deer season (also mating season), Bill saw it angling towards his blind and told this story when he came in. "I saw the cross-eyed buck by my blind at about 7:00 a.m. today. The sun was just starting to melt the frost off of the trees and first this doe came through the small popples. The heat waves were coming off of her too. She either had frost on her back or she was one hot Mama. She stopped and grazed and old cross-eyes spotted her. You guys know that he always sees two of everything. Well, I heard him grunting like he was getting friendly with that doe. With his double-vision, he saw the doe and a high pine stump that he mistook for another doe. He appeared like he was going to be real romantic and mate from a running start. He gave a sexy grunt, had his tongue hanging out a foot and charged! There was a loud crash! He jumped the stump thinking it was the doe! That guy must have had his 'personables' smart because you could hear him running hell bent for the creek. I heard him jump in and give a few grunts that didn't sound so romantic. Ya, if you guys don't believe that, I can show you the messed-up stump." Bill has a son that is a priest and he always reminds us of this after such an unusual story.

It seemed like one frustrated buck. Nothing went where he put it. He would also attempt to step over a log but would instead, step right on it. What seemed to really help him was that he had a keen nose and could smell his way around trouble.

We thought that he must travel a lot at night because we'd hear a crash in the woods here and a crash there. He has some real crazy moves like a sideways slide step when he sensed trouble and would run away. This makes him a hard target. Different camp members would come into the camp at night after "going to the toilet under the stars" and say they heard the cross-eyed buck, "busting brush" in the dark.

So far, none of the surrounding camps admit to having shot him. We'll be looking closely again this year for him or any "side-stepping offsprings" (if he was so lucky).

CHAPTER 21

ANTICIPATION OF NOVEMBER 15TH—
DEER SEASON OPENS
(November 14th—The Longest Day)

There are four, great, recognized, holidays in the U.P., Christmas, New Years, Easter, and Deer Season. They are all times of annual family and friends gathering. If you cannot attend one of these, particularly deer season, because of your job, military, etc. you call or write to receive all of the detail of the happenings.

In our camp, the action seems to start with the wood pile. We gather about three full cord, then pile it, cut, split, pile, move, pile, and pile it some more. Before we started to split, Bill said, "I know a camp that has a wood splitter. I'll go see if I can borrow it and save a lot of work." Dan perked up and said, "No, don't let him go. He did that to us last year and came back half in the bag, no splitter, and no booze for us." Bill said, "Ya, but I was thinking about you guys all of the time."

Scouting for deer sign, like ground scraps and tree rubs are priority along with well-used deer trails. One year, a friend (?) of Bill's took an iron bar and made a "look-alike" deer rub next to Bill's deer post. No one let on with that one and we still think he secretly brought corn out to that spot in anticipation.

Making new and repairing old deer blinds is next. We've got one camp member who finds the thickest woods with good deer sign and then proceeds to cut all of the woods out. Dan said, "I don't know, somehow his post doesn't look the same as before he clear-cut it." Someone will say, "what happened to those rolls of roofing paper we had for the blinds?" Dan will correct him and say, "what roofing paper? You didn't bring up anything new in five years." Then, "how about the beer I brought up? That doesn't count because it's all gone already." The mild frustrations are offset by the happiness of just being there.

The air is brisk. The first few snowflakes are in the air. Someone points out the flock of Canadian geese flying over. In no time, the woodpile is done and it's "Miller time." We all go inside and the wood heat feels good. Everyone's patting Dan on the back for bringing the Millers but as Bill cautions, "don't pat him too much because after it's gone it's not here anymore." Everyone agrees. The younger camp member, Don, looked at Bill like he had great wisdom. After a few rounds, the stories start to flow from last year's hunt. Remember when Bill was posting by that pond and that big one tried to jump over it and became stuck in it? Bill ejected all of his shells from his gun without firing a shot and as he tells us, he doesn't get Buck Fever. Remember Dad was sitting in the outhouse with the door wide open and that ten-pointer walked 30 feet away from him. I always said you have to take a rifle to the outhouse. Remember that smart eight-pointer that waited for the last poster to be placed on the deer drive, then doubled back into the second poster that he didn't hear stop off. There's his rack right up there.

The card playing starts. Smear is the name of the game at our camp. It's played for, who does the dishes, brings in the wood, money, and a general pastime. It's the kind of game that everyone can tell jokes and play at the same time. Bill was losing pretty steady. Dan, who was winning, looked at him and said, "you've got to be kind of intelligent to win at this." Bill looked back at him intently through bloodshot eyes and said, "you will never convince anyone on that point. Give Dan another Millers."

One year, we used a really worn-out deck of cards that were so sticky, we put flour on them to make them slide. We had flour on the table, on the cards, the floor, and up to our elbows by the time we quit.

The jokes told while playing cards are all in fun but some would not register a 1 on a 1 to 10 point scale. Dan reached way back on this one and said, "what is the name of a lady with one leg a foot shorter and the other one?" He stumped the group so he said, "I-lene. You know, guys, I-lene? Do you get it?" We all looked serious at him and talked about promoting him to camp cook for that one. Camp cook—a dreaded job. You're the target for the jokes and no compliments. Our standing rule is that if you complain about the cooking, you're the next cook. The comments normally sound like, "It tastes like hell—but it's good!"

ANTICIPATION—in checking the deer stands. Bill would always have two "hot spots" and would try to convince me into posting at one of them. He'd swear that someone would get a big buck there. It always seemed suspicious that he always wanted to go to the other one.

Everyone piles their clothes in a certain place in the camp so they aren't mixed with someone else's. Also, you then can place them in the order that you want to put them on so you don't forget a layer.

The day is running out and evening is fast in coming. The talk starts, "How many shells are you going to take with you tomorrow? Ten. What the hell, you're not that bad of a shot. Take five—that's lighter." I then notice Dan stick a whole box of 20 into his coat.

"When should we quit the post and come in to eat?" (We normally stick it out until 10:30 or if you hear a shot close by, we stay longer.)

Then, it's time for bed the night before the opener. It seems like being a kid again—like the night before Christmas. It's difficult to sleep. With the lights out, it's really dark. No street lights, no cars going by. You hear the wood stove crackling. A piece of wood drops down further in the stove with a thud as it burns. Dan fell asleep and is snoring real loud. After awhile, you think, God, I wish I could have fallen asleep before he started that. In the morning, you know he'll tell everyone that he couldn't sleep at all.

Someone gets up to relieve them self and the sounds keep repeating until daybreak. We're all up when the alarm rings at 5 a.m. Everyone dresses up, slow, so you don't skip a layer. We eat and start out for the deer post as you're ready. Going out the door, I smile as I hear someone saying, "wait you guys, I can't find my gloves. Who's got my gloves?" We all smile as we pass through the door. He always forgets something but at least he always brings a lot of beer.

CHAPTER 22

DEER BLINDS
AND CREATURE COMFORTS

One of my hunting partners and I applied for our deer hunting license today. That process really has changed over the years. We used to receive a metal-locking band that you locked around the deer's horn after you shot it. You could always tell who were the lucky hunters in the local "watering holes" during the season. The lucky one's had a smile and no tag showing. The others always had their tag twisted onto their hunting jacket pocket, cap, belt, or some other place handy to use when the time came.

Now, we receive a small piece of paper. We provide our own string to attach it to the deer and don't even need the traditional back tag displayed on your back while hunting. Nothing much to brag about with this new setup.

The license clerk punches into their computer, your name, address, hunting land tax number, other minor details, and then steps back and waits. The computer is now making sounds like it's digesting all of this. The clerk then tells you, "now we have to wait, the computer is working." You wonder what it is REALLY checking. Did you pay your land taxes this year? Do you go to church regularly? Do you take proper care of your garbage weekly? Are you a Republican or a Democrat? Do the Republicans get an extra license?

Finally, a slip of paper slowly comes out of the top of the computer (about the size of a grocery store receipt). She say's, "Don't lose this. It shows you also applied for the doe license. It's your only proof of your license, so don't misplace it."

At first, I'm happy. The computer must have given me a free pass for whatever it was checking. Then I wonder, where can I hide that flimsy, look-alike receipt to a grocery store printout so that my wife won't throw it away in her "forever cleaning" household ways. I decided to place it in that annual box of church envelopes. No one looks in there very often anyway.

Our next thoughts now turn to the deer blinds. The old ones always need repair and we normally like to make at least one new one in a different location per year. We hunt on three 40's. When we first started hunting here (Lake Township, Menominee County) years ago, our blinds consisted of sitting as still as possible against a big tree with no other cover. We later placed brush around where we sat to give a blind effect. You could then move your feet without showing motion to a watchful deer. I sat so quiet in this type of blind that chickadees would land on my gun barrel and walk its length while looking you in the eyes and not be disturbed.

Ben made one of these type blinds one year out of cedar boughs. It wasn't the smartest move. Deer love to eat cedar boughs. The first day, a fork-horn buck came from behind him, stuck its head into his blind and quietly ate cedar. He was sitting about two feet away from the deer's head. I don't really know what Ben did but he didn't shoot at the deer. He walked back to the camp kind of odd-like and changed his underwear.

Then, one year, we all got good and wet on a rainy first day. The next year, we built roofs over the top of the blinds. It was a pleasure to sit in those during a snowstorm and watch a brown deer sneaking along through the white snow.

Last year, I saw 19 chickadees, 2 blue jay, 8 squirrels, 2 partridge, and 4 flocks of geese flying over. That really is a thrilling sound. I feel very special to be in the woods in the U.P. when I can hear and see the geese fly over. I also saw a fork-horn buck and a doe an hour later. They both went to see their maker. I couldn't help but believe that they were happier to meet up with my 30/30 rather than a car bumper.

There seems to always be some interesting stories that come in from the blinds. I went to our "swamp blind" before daylight last year. You couldn't see anything in it except the bench seat. I sat down and about five minutes later, the leaves under the seat began to rustle loudly and a porcupine ran out from under there. Those were a few tense moments.

Two years ago, Ben fell asleep in his blind. He had his rifle standing along side of him in there. Bill checked on him to see how he was doing. When he discovered Ben was sleeping, he reached in and took his rifle back to the camp. Ben looked pretty bewildered when he came into camp without his rifle.

Last year, Dave was in his blind about 100 yards distance from a county road. It was the first day and he was quiet, happy, and hopeful. About 9 a.m., he said, a car stopped on the road and a woman walked in by his blind and asked him if this road went into Stephenson. He said, "Lady, why did you come in here to see ME?" She said, "because she saw his orange coat and thought she'd ask because she wasn't sure where she was." She said, "What are you hunting out here?" He said he was tempted to ease back the hammer.

The best blind that I have seen belongs to a neighboring camp. My friend, Gene, can build anything and is really creative. He has a completely enclosed blind, insulated walls, coffee pot, a working TV with the ear plug connection, a heater, swivel chair, and so help me, a tall TV antenna. The antenna is an arm's distance out the back window. He has a large pipe wrench attached to it like a handle. He said, "to change major channels, I reach out and give the pipe wrench a turn and get clear reception." I told him, he should feel somewhat ashamed of himself in there so comfortable when his wife thinks he's freezing under a tree somewhere waiting for a deer. He gave me a big smile and said proudly, "Ya, I really feel bad about this."

I said, "If Daniel Boone could come back and see how we hunt deer now." Gene thought for awhile and said, "Hell, if Daniel Boone could come back now, he'd probably want to go in town and get a hamburger and a beer, which is what I think we should do." It was always hard to disagree with Gene.

Vic, the newest hunter in camp, asked what do we do after we fix the blinds? I said, "then we tackle that wood pile and later I'll take you over to meet Gene. You won't believe the deer blind he has. Some guys just don't hunt like we do anymore. They like it a lot more comfortable, I guess."

CHAPTER 23

MENOMINEE COUNTY TURKEY HUNT
(Or—Not Everyone Gets the Bird)

I was up to my camp a few weekends ago. It was early morning with the start of a light rain. I was beginning to see turkeys during the rain. Two at the edge of a field, four walked across a gravel road, and when I turned into my camp road, two turkeys were walking down it toward my camp.

I got out of my pickup, quietly unlocked the road cable and drove in behind them. The road is about two hundred yards long. They walked in about 30 feet in front of the truck, then walked into the woods. As long as I didn't scare them, they just walked slowly away.

My experience has been that they are more active and come out near the roads during a rain. Ben, somehow, had heard about what I had seen on this trip. He came over to my house and invited me to go hunting with him. He was an accomplished hunter and said I'd have a lot of fun watching him call one in and besides, it's beautiful in the woods now (no mosquitoes, etc.).

I agreed to go with him on the following weekend. This would be my first experience watching a confident turkey hunter. He said, "Don't be concerned about a lunch. I'll have enough lunch for the both of us. All you have to do is help watch for an "in-coming" turkey.

I asked him where he planned on hunting. "I thought we'd hunt the back end of your land. All indications seem to be that turkeys would be there," he said. I figured, that explains why he invited me to go with on this hunt.

Driving up, he said, "I've got a good decoy, a new $20.00 box-call and a big lunch. If we see any, this could be an exciting day." I asked him to stop at my friend, John's home (John lives about 7 miles from my camp.) He is a native of the area and an accomplished hunter of whatever moves. We could ask him about some pointers, locations, for getting a turkey up there.

We were visiting in his front room when we brought up the subject. "Turkeys?" he said. "If you want to see some, I'll call a few right up to the porch." Ben looked at me, like, "Yeah, sure." The house had a lawn and open fields around it for at least a good 80 yards before you entered any woods.

"You don't have to spend a lot of money on a turkey call," he said. "I use this plastic, gallon, milk jug with a handful of loose corn in it." Ben started to shake, like, he had a start of a good belly laugh coming.

We all went on the front porch and John began to shake that milk jug. I have to admit that it looked unbelievable, but I knew John well enough that I started to look for the turkeys.

Within two-three minutes, a line of turkeys came running out of the woods up to his house. When turkeys run full-speed (about 25 mph), it's a sight to see. John then threw some loose corn down for them to eat and we went into the house and watched them through the window.

Ben slowly pulled his box call out of his pocket and stared at it. I could just imagine what he was thinking. "I paid $20.00 for THIS?" John said that he conditioned the birds to that sound every time that he fed them. Ben began to ask, "Could we . . . (and John cut him off with), "No you can't. I don't shoot at these. They are like pets and we enjoy watching them."

When we left, Ben was grumbling in the truck, "Pets, hell. The DNR never said anything about pets." We got to my land and, true to form, when you tell someone that there is game around, you see nothing.

Ben found the spot that he liked, set up his decoy and we settled down to wait. He said, "Let's eat the lunch before the action starts." So he opened the lunch bag and pulled out a sandwich for each of us. Big baloney and plain bread. No butter or mustard. Nothing extra. He smiled and said, "Eat up, I got a lot of these." Before I could ask what did he have to drink, he said, "I had a six-pack ready to go but I forgot it at home." The baloney was fresh though, and somehow, it tasted twice as good as it would have at home.

There was turkey sign around us when you looked harder. Turkey droppings on the road and dusting areas (although that could have been a partridge OR a turkey.)

We were quiet for a long time as Ben worked that $20.00 (plus tax) box call like he meant it. It was either a coincidence or good calling but a red fox came sneaking through. It was close enough to shoot.

We heard blue jays, sand cranes flying over, THEN . . . ! We heard the first gobble—then another! Ben was working that call, "cluck, cluck, cluck, cluck." The turkey seemed to actually answer, "cluck, cluck, cluck," but it wouldn't come out of the dense woods that it was in.

I leaned over to Ben and whispered, "We should have that "milk jug" call. It seems like yours is scaring it away." Ben looked at me kind of blank, then, looked the same way at the $20.00 call box. Then he looked up to the sky like he was doing some deep thinking. I was convinced, as dumb as it may sound, that he would try a "milk-jug" call the next time.

We didn't get any turkey but the baloney sandwiches (3-4 slices thick) were good and as I reminded him, he owes me a beer.

CHAPTER 24

HUNTING WITH ELIZABETH—
A HOT PARTNER

So, your wife bought you a portable gas heater to take deer hunting, right? This should keep you warmer and you can enjoy the hunt more. Not necessarily so. One of our camp members brought one to camp this year with that in mind.

The idea sounded good. The heater looked good—the kind that screws onto the top of a portable bottle gas can. He had a 10 gallon gas can which then wasn't too heavy to carry.

He said, "Guys, I'm not going to freeze this year. When you have to leave your posts because you're cold, I'll be able to sit and see more deer." Sound good? Sounded good to us. We were starting to entertain thoughts like, hope he gets diarrhea and he'll have to stay in camp so we can use it.

He proudly put it together in camp the night before season. Everything fit well. Nice brass fittings to tighten up. Then he opened the valve and with a match, lit it up. The heater's head-piece immediately turned a bright orange-red color from the heat and it made a somewhat loud sizzling sound like, SH, SHHHHHHHH! We said that the sound it makes will keep the deer away. You might be warm, but the deer will make a wide circle around you.

Bill said, "I don't think so. They aren't that afraid of cars on the road are they?" Well, he had a point, so we thought like any other new thing we tried at camp, give him a chance. Being that its color was all silver, he brought an old, red, flannel shirt and buttoned it over the tank. The top of the heater part stuck out above like a small kid's head. He had gotten a red, knit, women's winter hat at a garage sale from a woman's house named Elizabeth. He put the cap over the heater-head. Now, he had a safe, colored heater to carry through the woods. He called it, "Elizabeth" after the lady he bought the hat from.

The first day, he was taking "Elizabeth" out to his deer blind. It looked like he was carrying a little kid by the back of the neck as he was disappearing into the dark woods (we've got some unusual guys at our camp).

He told us that he got to his blind and "fired up Elizabeth." He said the heater-head's bright glow caused a light and the SHHHHH ... sound of the burner was very noticeable in the quiet woods.

He heard deer but didn't see any so he figured he had to improvise that heater better and hide the light and sound. He had a flannel blanket on his folding chair that he was sitting on. He took the heater, placed it close to him, and covered it and his lap with the blanket. It cut the light way down and did muffle the sound from the bottle gas.

He said, "Boys, after awhile, I was really comfortable. The heat under there started to feel like I was in a sauna!" He turned in his seat a little, and the blanket started to slip down. He said he fixed that by tying the blanket around his waist with his deer pulling rope.

After all of this, about an hour later, a buck started coming his way but off to the side of him. He turned to line up for the shot and he could instantly smell something hot and burning! His blanket slipped into the heater-head and started a fire.

"What would you do, guys?" he said. "Put out the fire or concentrate on getting that buck?" He glanced at the fire and it didn't look that bad so he shot at the buck. He did get the buck and by then that flannel blanket was pretty much ablaze.

He rolled on the ground to put it out and was lucky that only the blanket and the seat of his hunting pants was the only things burned. That was quite a story when he got back to camp. He volunteered, "Does anyone want to take Elizabeth out to your deer blind tomorrow?" We all said, "No-o-o-o-o, she's a little too hot for us."

CHAPTER 25

TO GRUNT OR NOT TO GRUNT
A Report of This Year's Deer Camp

This was an extra good year at our deer camp (1997). I hesitate to tell you exactly where it is in Menominee County. The DNR may read this and next year, start a special, SPECIAL, season there.

We saw more deer at camp this year than we have in the last 15 years. They were also extra "spooky." The slightest sound seemed to set them off moving away. They were also very hesitant to come into a bait pile. Those that did, had their ears moving every which way. They ate very little and moved out quickly.

The first morning, I was in my blind about a half hour before daylight. I had all of the "good" baits out in front of me. Apples, pumpkins, and a good buck lure. How do I know the buck lure was good? Well, two nights before season, my brother, Bill, opened the lure bottle and took a good whiff of it. His eyes kind of floated to the top of his head and he immediately started to make excuses why he had to go home that night to visit his wife. We made a big joke of it and convinced him to stay at camp. He tossed and turned something frightful all night so we thought, that must be some powerful stuff!

The wind was blowing all of these enticing smells down into the swamp that my blind overlooked. Right at 7:15 a.m., a huge buck came walking out of the swamp in a direct line to me. He came about a third of the distance between us. I had my gun only half way to my shoulder as he was looking directly at me. Then, he turned quickly to the left into a thick group of spruce trees and was gone.

What started out to be a "shooting fish in a barrel shot" turned out to be really disappointing. I don't think that buck ever saw me. He just naturally was going to use that trail. It's hard to see one so easily and not be able to get a shot at it.

That afternoon, a doe and about a four-inch spike horn came to the bait pile and stayed a long time. I passed it up thinking I was going to be up to the camp for two weeks and should see a bigger one. There were at least one to four does there every day thereafter.

I took my friend, Don, from Stephenson to my blind late in the season and showed him what happened with that big buck on the first day. He said, "You need a grunt call. I grunted a nice buck in on the first day. Without grunting, I'd never have gotten it."

Who said there isn't always something new that a poor deer hunter can't buy? I heard about the grunt calls before but until someone who I knew well could vouch for its success, I never took it seriously.

This year, we had a nonresident guest hunter in camp. We posted him on a different corner of the 40. If I had to bet on it, I would have said that spot should have been good for at least two bucks. He brought a pair of deer antlers with him. He felt he could bring in a buck with them. The first day, he started to bang those antlers together to lure one in. I could hear him banging away over by my post. His pattern sounded like a polka beat—dee-da-dee-deet, dee-da-dee-deet, dee-da-dee-dee-dee-da-deet-deet. And it was LOUD!

First, I saw two partridge flying away from that area. Then, a rabbit and three blue jays came fleeing like running from a forest fire with fear in their eyes! Lord knows what the deer thought.

Being that he wouldn't quit, I took a walk over there and told him quietly, no more of that. "You're scaring everything away." He smiled and said, "I'm just getting warmed up!" I said, "You might be getting warmed up but you've got the deer dancing over to the next 40's."

Bill came to my blind at noon. I couldn't help but notice his nose twitch when he smelled that deer lure. He said, "I heard that racket way over by me too. If he does that again, we should tie those antlers onto his head and let him make a drive on the state 40's. Those guys over there are real jumpy." Kelley said, "I don't think I scared anything." Just then, a pumpkin that he had sitting on a stump fell off with a thud as it hit the ground. Bill said, "Look at that. The pumpkin is even trying to get away." Kelly commented, "These deer up here (Menominee County) aren't used to these modern hunting aides." Bill, with a gleam in his eye, looked back at him and said, "Did you ever make a deer drive using those antlers? I'll bet you could really get something going."

Kelly looked back at him like, "These U.P. rednecks couldn't have ever read an Outdoor Life magazine." I asked, "How many deer did you see this morning?" "None," he said. "I think you put me in a poor spot."

There were 11 tree rubs and 1 ground scrape all within 30 yards from his blind. Normally, he should have gotten the first buck.

My neighbor, Gene's, camp has one member that snores big time! They made a blind for him in their swamp. When he falls asleep, they can hear him way up in the popples on the high land, soon as he starts snoring, they all sit at "high alert" because deer will normally come sneaking out of the swamp. They claim it works as good as a deer drive. That camp owns seven 40's. They weren't shooting anything under six points. They also had high success.

The second week, I walked slowly up to my blind and looked down to check if any deer were at the bait pile. Like we've done a hundred times before and never saw any. This time, there was a nice fork horn buck eating there. I ended his appetite for pumpkins with one shot. Brother Bill missed one buck on opening day but connected with a fork horn on the third day. His son missed two bucks and we all saw a lot of does.

When I got home, I told my wife all about the deer grunting and that I need a grunt call for next year. She said, "How does it sound?" I demonstrated, like this, "wwwh, wwwh, WWWH!" She said, "Just like that?" "We-l-l-l, yeah," I replied. She smiled and said, "Then you don't need one. You already grunt like an old buck."

My poor wife just doesn't know how to play the game—or does she?

CHAPTER 26

THE DAY SOME L.P. HUNTERS
TRIED TO TAKE OVER OUR DEER BLINDS

In our hunting area, everyone respects property
rights and tries to use common sense with others.
We have our own camps, camp land to hunt, and do
hunt some parts of state 40's bordering us. All
camps have done this for years.

The camp next to us had two blinds made on a state
40 joining their own camp land. The blinds were
about 20 feet into the state land from their own.
These were not permanent blinds but anyone with
hunting sense could tell that they were freshly redone
for use.

We don't see too many strangers where we hunt
because most of the land is privately owned by the
same camp owners for many years. The day before
this season, there were two Lower Peninsula hunters
sitting in these 'state blinds.' They found them and
gave the appearance of holding them for the season.
They started to bait where there already was a bait
pile.

Two of this camp's younger hunters discovered them.
The younger guys were promptly told to leave. They
told them that this was a state 40 and they were

sitting in these blinds. Most of us know that the law states, no permanent blinds on state land to eliminate just this type of problem.

The boys ran back to camp, all out of breath, to tell the rest that some strangers were taking over these blinds. After they got the whole story, everyone wanted to do something different to solve it. Don, the camp owner, said, "No, to remove the blinds at night will only upset them AND US. We'll try a little diplomacy. Big Bob, you're elected. I want you to go over and talk to those guys and be sure they understand. If they argue, be sure to tell them something convincing. I'm sure you can handle this if everyone keeps cool. We'll stand by the camp door. If something goes real sour, give us a holler. We'll hear you."

Bob said, he knew he had backup. He said he approached them from behind and to one side. (Bob, I would imagine, was given the job because he goes between 290-350 pounds of solid muscle. He worked at a local dairy for many years, "throwing 20 gallon milk cans around all day" and he looked the part.) He said they started by arguing about free hunting on state 40's and that they had possession of these blinds. Bob said, "I don't remember everything I told them, but when they thought they had the run on the talking, I reached over and broke a four-inch popple tree in half with my two hands." He said, he smiled and told them he suffered from post traumatic stress syndrome (some big words Bob said he read in camp from the DNR about the suffering deer herd). He told them, he got this in the war. He also told them that most everyone in the camp is a veteran with something different wrong with them (they were all veteran hunters). He said, "You're lucky that the guy that got sprayed with that orange stuff didn't come to see you. You know, we never know where he goes in the morning when he goes outside for a toilet break. Sometimes, he doesn't come back for a couple of hours."

Bob said, being diplomatic, I told them of some other state 40's that they could hunt without problems and closer to the road so they wouldn't get lost. "I think I convinced them," Bob told the story with a smile. "They gave me a bag of deer apples and our two hot seats that they found in the blinds." What really convinced them? I think what did it was when I leaned real close to them and said, in the low voice that he uses all the time, "If I saw their car parked by the end of the camp 40 again, he'd personally tip it over." He looks like he could probably do it, too.

They thanked him and said that they wanted to leave to find a new spot to hunt before dark. They said he was one of the nicest "Yoopers" that they talked to in the woods.

Bob said he told them that, "you know, most of you 'Trolls' are good sportsmen. You just have to stop and ask people what's open to hunt and show that you want to cooperate." They shook their heads and agreed.

CHAPTER 27

NEVER FOOL WITH BABE

Our camp members got an early-in-the-day start to go up to check out the camp this last March. Other than a big meal cooked over the wood stove, there wasn't really much excitement that we were looking forward to. A few deer tracks, snow, and muddy roads didn't give much promise of an exciting trip.

We thought we'd stop at the local bar and check out what was happening lately. This stop is normally as good as a newspaper is downtown. You just have to be patient and listen.

The bar was about half full. We found four seats on one end, ordered beer, and looked around. A run-of-the-mill crowd of locals. It seemed like most of them were there just to be near other people. Living in the woods can be lonely.

We all noticed this heavy-set woman dressed in "logger's clothes" sitting at the bar by herself. Vic said, "She covered the whole stool well and then some but not with any fat." The locals, sitting near her (this was a very long bar), seemed to give her whatever room she wanted as there was an empty stool on each side of her.

She had a beer and a couple of hamburgers with raw onions. This was about 8:30 in the morning so we figured that she must be one tough logger! She looked to be well-respected by the locals and on her own, probably was a very nice, hard-working person.

Our guys started to talk about her among themselves. "I'll bet she could cut a cord of wood with the chain saw turned off." "I'd hate to come home late at night and have to face her."

As we were watching her, all of a sudden, she let out a loud sound, like, AAAAAH! Automatically, all the locals slid down one extra stool on either side of her. They hardly looked up, like, this was routine and time to give her space.

We couldn't see anything that happened but we started to guess. She might have hit a nerve from a bad tooth (toothache). She might not have slept inside last night. She might be irritated by someone's cologne (it didn't seem like she used any deodorant), or maybe she had too many raw onions. Then, the jiving seemed to quit all at once. After all, she was one of us. A real U.P. survivor.

The "bar news" was next to nothing. "Do you know County Road 362 is softening up on the hills? It's really getting muddy." The bartender was telling me that he couldn't wait to go home and sleep. He drove to Marquette last night for the basketball playoffs and was dead tired.

All was quiet up and down the bar. Then the "logging lady" started to argue with some guy near her. The bartender said to me, "God, I hope she doesn't start anything. I'm tired, dragged-out, and I don't need this." Almost at the same time, three guys (about 25-30 years old) came in.

Right away, you could tell that they were probably from Chicago by their dress, boisterous ways, and their conversation. They were LOUD! They seemed to WANT attention. Then they started to "poke fun" at the sports decor in the tavern. Oh, Oh! This looked like real trouble. This probably was a second home for most everyone here. It bothered US.

The three of them were drinking and the middle one seemed to have a hard time standing up, and they were snickering. The middle guy said, loudly, "I can beat the hell out of anyone in here." They were young, well-built, and probably believed that. It's always easy for someone to act brave when they are one of a crowd.

The bartender said, "Geeze! I've got Babe ready to explode and now these jokers come in looking for a fight."

Babe turned around on her stool and looked at them through half-closed eyes. You could see that she was ugly and she knew it. She was tough and she knew it. She seemed very confident and proud that she was tough. Bill even whispered to me, "Man, that's one tough Mama."

She propped an elbow onto the bar, rolled a toothpick around in her mouth and half smiled. When Vic saw that smile, he said he looked behind us for the back door. I figured, THIS IS IT! The moment of truth! Sizing things up, I was happy that I wasn't from Chicago. It looked like it could be real messy.

Just as I was starting to feel sorry for the bartender, he came up with a stroke of genius. He walked over to the side of the bar near Babe and said, in a normal voice, "Take these guys outside, will you Babe?"

She walked over to them and smiled. You could tell that they never expected a woman to confront them. The three of them seemed to realize that all three of them, together, could lose a fight with her. She was standing about two feet in front of them. For whatever crazy reason, the middle guy gave her a hard punch in the belly. His fist seemed to bounce back. She was braced and ready for them.

Smiling at them, all the time, she reached up behind two of them, locked onto their hair, and turned their heads skyward. She said, "Are you KIDS ready to leave?" They all meekly moved along with her.

There is a long, sloping, ramp for the handicapped coming into this bar. I suppose it was with some satisfaction, she flipped the "stomach puncher" over the ramp's railing when she let them go. They left quickly!

When she came back in, the bartender said, "Babe drinks free for the rest of the day." She rolled that toothpick around in her mouth and said, "And I'll have a few more of them hamburgers."

CHAPTER 28

BUCK FEVER AND BEN

There is such a thing as "Buck Fever!" I always thought that it was just an expression until I saw it firsthand.

Four of us were hunting out of a small deer camp in the Jimtown area near Cedar River, Michigan. When I say it was small, it had two double bunks, a table, a stove, chairs, and a mirror inside. Anything else that you wanted to do, you went outside. Washing up on a snowy porch was a new experience. Inside, if you took three steps in any direction from the bunks, it seemed as though you were by a wall. It had characteristics of a tent. It was small, cold, and the roof leaked.

We were three young hunters with our veteran hunter and Grandfather with us. He was an excellent sportsman and a good teacher for beginners.

Well, it was the night before opening day. We were all cleaning our guns and talking over where we each would "post" for deer. Then, at 10:30 a.m., we'd meet and make a few deer drives. The drives accomplished two things. We might possibly chase out a few deer to whoever was on the "stand" at the end of the drives. It also warmed us up from sitting so long in the cold.

Back to the Buck Fever. The first day, Ben and I posted about 10 acres apart from each other. I sat as long as I could until my feet became really cold. As Ben was only a short distance away, I heard no shooting from him so I decided to slow-walk toward him and possibly see a moving deer.

As I came into sight of him, I saw something unusual. Ben was standing up and aiming his gun downhill at a deer. The barrel of his gun was moving steady in about a six inch circle. Once in awhile, he'd shove the gun forward about a foot as he was aiming. He never fired a shot. I saw the deer below him but there was no way I could safely shoot past him so he had to do it himself.

Finally, the deer walked away and into a cedar swamp. Ben was sweating. His eyes were open wide like he was giving birth to a baby. He told me that he saw a nice buck but just couldn't get a good shot. I saw the deer grazing below him peacefully for 3-5 minutes.

I thought to myself, so that's what they must call "Buck Fever." Becoming so excited that you freeze up and don't function normally.

Then, at 10:30 a.m., we all met to begin the deer drives. Ben and I were the drivers on this particular one. We walked parallel to each other to "push out" whatever we could to our "standers." After a few minutes, a nice buck ran ahead of Ben. It ran directly toward a pond and jumped in. I'm sure it wanted to cross the pond and escape on the other side. As luck would have it, it's front legs drove down deep into the pond's muddy bottom and it became stuck there.

Picture a nice eight-point buck offering a shot like that. Ben ran up to approximately 30 feet from it, placed his lever action 30/30 up to his shoulder and proceeded to aim at the deer and eject all five shells that he had in the gun onto the ground.

The deer was struggling for "deer life" and finally became free and cleared out of there. Ben said his sights must be off because he never hit the deer.

I showed him the pile of shells that he ejected without shooting. He couldn't believe it! The next day, as he was returning to camp before dark, he heard sounds of brush cracking on the other side of some evergreen trees. Believing they were from a deer, he shot through the trees 2-3 times. He, of course didn't get a deer there.

That evening, I didn't return to the camp until after dark. There were some anxious moments in camp until I walked in. Grandpa was a good, patient person who was tolerant of beginners but he also had a fondness for living.

The next night, Ben came in on the end of the day with cold hands and was going to eject his shells from his gun onto the bed. BOOM! That was an exceptionally loud shot in that small camp as Ben's cold finger touched the trigger.

We were all facing different directions and we all instantly started "patting ourselves down" to see if we were shot. Grandpa, our camp leader and recognized boss, turned around to face Ben. He asked, "Where did that shot go?"

Ben said, "Through the blankets, mattress, and I think, through the floor." Gramps calmly said, "I think you had better pack up now and go back home tonight. We'll see about hunting with you next year."

Ben never hesitated. He packed up quickly. I think he must have scared himself as much as he scared us. Buck Fever IS real and dangerous.

CHAPTER 29

DEER AND WINE DON'T MIX

The Italian camps in the Iron Mountain-Sagola area are all noted for their basic deer season requirements: spaghetti and meat balls and red wine.

Some of them take great pride in making their own wine. Are these wines made from backyard grapes? No sir! Unknown to many people, a group of Italians will contract with a California grape grower for red and white wine grapes. These have to be guaranteed to have a designated amount of alcohol content measured in them when they are harvested.

Each wine maker contracts for whatever amount of pounds he wants (or can afford). The grapes are then sent by full boxcars to Iron Mountain for their pick up and use. These wines are normally made in the home basements where some have actual wine cellars (dirt floors in them and the "right" temperature).

Part of the wine making process is placing the bunches of grapes and stems through a wine press. Turning the pressure down on the grapes makes the juice run off for use and you end up with a large "cake" of mash compressed tight together. Depending upon the size of the wine press, most "cakes" of compressed mash can be 6-8" thick and 2' in diameter. When this whole process is completed, the local wine maker has some "bragging stuff" or could have an expensive batch of vinegar. That's the test of a quality, Italian, wine maker.

Some of the pre-deer season excitement in my father-in-law's camp (100% Italian) was "Nardi is going to donate a gallon of his red wine for the first week," or "Vampa's promised to bring up a small barrel of that white wine that he made this year." "We all know how good THAT is from that card party at his house this October."

A meal to them with a nice glass of premium homemade wine is like a slice of Heaven. Then there was always a cleanup chore with the wine mash until, one day, Paulo had an unusual thought. He said that each camp feeds apples and corn to the deer, just maybe the deer would like that wine mash.

The camp that put this out REALLY had a story to tell. It seems that they took two "cakes" of wine mash to camp, broke it into four pieces each and placed it out for the deer. They came back a few days later to check if the deer ate it. When they drove up to the camp, they automatically looked down toward the deer-bait pile. "It was a sight to see," said Paulo. There were eight deer sitting on the ground within 20 feet from the wine mash. We looked at them and they just looked back at us while they were chewing their cuds. They never made a move to jump up and run away.

Paulo said, "After we sized up the situation, we guessed they may have had a 'hangover' from eating that wine mash." They then walked up to one and touched it on its hind quarter with a foot. The deer then stood up on wobbly legs and wobbled about 10 feet and sat down again. It just looked back at them.

Smugger, Paulo's partner, said, "Those deer had a first-class 'jag' on. They were 'stoned,' and 'pickled.'"

Then a neighboring camp to them, not to be outdone by that wine mash experience, decided to try and capture a live deer off of the apple-bait pile. They dug a hole deep enough to put a two-gallon pail in. Then, they filled it half full of apples.

They then took a TV antenna wire, made a noose on one end and placed it over the pail. The other end was run into the camp by a hole under the picture window on that side. They had a two foot piece of 2 x 4 tied to the end inside the camp.

Why they wanted to catch a live deer wasn't certain. They just wanted to see if they could do it. Little did they realize the problems they were going to create for themselves.

They said that this one evening about 5:00 p.m. a doe came to the pile, began eating apples, stuck its head into the bucket to eat and they pulled the wire! They soon discovered that they had about 150 pounds of pure explosion on their hands. They said that they took hold of the wire and tried to pull the deer toward the camp. The deer charged toward the picture window and they thought it was a goner. Then, the deer ran the length of the cable way from the camp. They said the cable "screamed" through their hands so fast that it took the skin off from inside of them.

The deer then made another run to the camp. They said by now, they were smart enough to not hold onto the wire. It then ran away from the camp much to their relief with thoughts of it jumping through that picture window.

The wire "sang" again as it was so quickly pulled back out the hole under the window. The 2 x 4 on the end of the cable slammed against the wall.

Finally, the deer sat down and with two long poles, they managed to free the deer from the noose and it ran away. Why did they do it? They said, just to see if they could catch one with no afterthought of what would happen after it was caught. They had the sore hands to support their story. The red wine flowed steady when that story is retold.

CHAPTER 30

OUT BIGGEST BUCK
AND MOST UNUSUAL HUNT

If your deer camp is in business for enough years, someone will eventually shoot a "bragging" buck. Our's happened some years ago during a BUCKS ONLY season.

This was an unusual hunting year for us. A new logging road was just pushed into what was before, a long-walk area, if you wanted to hunt it. Previously, we were hesitant to hunt back that far from our camp because of the distant walk before daylight, and if you shot a deer that far back, it was a long pull to bring it in.

Dad and I decided that we'd take the "camp car" halfway back there and walk the rest of the way on opening morning.

We were on our way at 5:00 a.m. that November 15th. There was no snow but one could see a lot of tracks crossing that new road. This was an area near the Menominee River and populated with a lot of oak trees. The acorns were plentiful. There was a lot of deer rubs and conditions looked good.

Dad found a giant pine tree stump burned black on the outside with all of the inside wood rotted away. He hollowed this out more and had a good "stand up" blind as the stump was about shoulder high. He was close enough to see the river from this stand.

My blind was about 20 acres away from his. It was sitting on top of a huge spruce tree that a windstorm must have uprooted out of the ground. Three good trails intersected about 30 yards in front of me through some young popples. A stream (about 10 feet across) ran parallel to me and five feet farther away than these trails. One trail looked like it went into the stream and across to the other side into a six-foot high, wild hay marsh.

Being that this new road started through our land and continued a good mile back to start logging on this state land, no other hunters were in this immediate area.

What a beautiful setting. We were on our posts before daylight. The sun's rays were just making color in the sky. You could hear blue bills whistling overhead, either coming or going to the river.

Then, just at daylight (enough to see your gun sights), I heard brush cracking from 2-3 deer running behind me and to my right. I thought, with the curve in the river, there was a good chance that they'd run up that trail Dad was watching. Boom! Boom! Boom! Three shots erupted the morning quiet coming from Dad's post. I braced myself for a possible shot if something turned my way.

A half hour later, Dad came to my post with a big smile and excitement in his eyes and said, "I missed a nice one." He then headed back to his tree blind for a possible second chance. An hour passed. I was seeing nothing but gray squirrels and a partridge walking around in front of me. Sitting as quiet as I was, I started to shake from the cold and lack of movement. My eyes were flickering between open and shut.

Boom! Then a 30 second silence and boom! again from Dad's post. I almost jumped off of the tree that I was sitting on from the unexpected noise. I figured he had one now for sure and the second, delayed shot must have finished it off.

A good 15 minutes later, he again came to my post and said, "I missed ANOTHER one! This one was bigger yet. Nice horns! Lots of horns!" I said, "Why don't you stay on your post now until 11:00 a.m. and maybe I'll get a shot." He was hunting with that long barreled 32 Special (mentioned in Chapter 10) and claimed that he couldn't see the end sight well. The rest of the story was that the first one ran past him about 30 feet away. The second one ran past about 15 yards away. He shot from the hip, missed, it ran about 50 feet and stood and looked back at him. He missed it again.

The next weekend, we were on the same posts. At about 7:15 a.m., a beautiful eight-point buck came walking out in front of me on one of those trails. I was shooting a 30/40 Krag. The wind was right so I let it walk and turn his head away from me. I sighted onto his front shoulder, shot, and that deer never moved. He slowly looked back and forth and stood there as if nothing happened. I eased back the bolt, popped up another shell, sighted him again, pulled the trigger and NOTHING HAPPENED! I slowly opened the breech, checked that there really was a new shell in the chamber, eased the bolt shut and pulled the trigger again. Nothing. The gun did not fire. Now, the deer started to walk away slowly into the creek and walked into the hay marsh out of sight.

As I pulled the hammer back about three times when attempting to fire that last shot, I thought I must have a broken firing pin.

Dad walked over and we reran the story. He said let me see the shell in your barrel. He discovered the firing pin entered neatly into the shell like it should have. The shell itself, was a dud. It just refused to fire.

In the excitement of quietly opening and closing my gun, checking if there was a new bullet and doing this so quietly that the deer didn't hear me, I never thought of a dud bullet to try another one.

We checked for blood and found blood and white hair stuck to a popple tree on the far side where the deer was standing when I shot. Tracking it in the marsh, we found two places where it laid down (was blood in it's bed), but without any snow and such a dense marsh, we lot its track.

The last weekend of the season, Dad and Big Bob (one of Dad's best friends) again went back there for a final hunt. They said that they arrived late at camp, went as quickly as they could to these way-back posts. It was getting too dark for them to walk into the posts so they each picked a corner of the skid trail away from each other and watched a fair section of the road hoping one would cross.

Dad said, "It was getting darker so that in five minutes more, you couldn't see to shoot." (He now had a 300 Savage with a two and a half power scope). "I heard a loud noise of a big animal coming out of the woods, confident in the darker light, coming out to cross the road. When it got near the road, I could see big horns and a huge, near-black deer. It looked as big as a horse. He stepped onto the skid trail, I got one shot with the cross hairs on his shoulder. It ran across and out of sight. I listened and heard a crash. He either knocked down a dead tree or crashed into some others. I knew I had him, then."

"Big Bob came over with his flashlight and we found it right where I heard the crashing sound. It was a 14-point buck with two of the long tines broken off probably from a fight with another buck." Dad continued, "No offense, but I was glad Big Bob was with me rather than you. He dragged it out himself and put it up on the car fender with no problem." We estimated that it weighed in at 225#.

We still have that 14-pointer's rack hanging in the camp. Strangers still ask where and how did we get it?